The
American Institute of International Law:

Its Declaration of the Rights and Duties of Nations

By

JAMES BROWN SCOTT
President of the American Institute of International Law

Le premier et le plus grand intérêt est toujours la justice. Tous veulent que les conditions soient égales pour tous, et la justice n'est que cette égalité. Le citoyen ne veut que les lois et que l'observation des lois. Chaque particulier dans le peuple sait bien que, s'il y a des exceptions, elles ne seront pas en sa faveur. Ainsi tous craignent les exceptions; et qui craint les exceptions aime la loi.

JEAN JACQUES ROUSSEAU.

With a new introduction by William E. Butler
John Edward Fowler Distinguished Professor of Law,
Pennsylvania State University;
Academician, National Academy of Sciences of Ukraine and
Russian Academy of Natural Sciences

THE LAWBOOK EXCHANGE, LTD.
Clark, New Jersey

ISBN-13: 9781616190316 (hardcover)
ISBN-13: 9781616190323 (paperback)
Lawbook Exchange edition 2010

Frontis portrait of James Brown Scott with permission of
Carnegie Endowment for International Peace

The quality of this reprint is equivalent to the quality of the original work.

THE LAWBOOK EXCHANGE, LTD.
33 Terminal Avenue
Clark, New Jersey 07066-1321

*Please see our website for a selection of our other publications
and fine facsimile reprints of classic works of legal history:*
www.lawbookexchange.com

Library of Congress Cataloging-in-Publication Data

Scott, James Brown, 1866-1943.
  The American Institute of International Law : its Declaration of
the Rights and Duties of Nations / by James B. Scott ; with a
new introduction by William E. Butler.
      p. cm.
  Originally published: Washington, D.C. : American Institute of
International Law, 1916 (LCCN: 19-018675)
  Includes bibliographical references.
   ISBN-13: 978-1-61619-031-6 (cloth : alk. paper)
   ISBN-10: 1-61619-031-0 (cloth : alk. paper)
   ISBN-13: 978-1-61619-032-3 (pbk. : alk. paper)
   ISBN-10: 1-61619-032-9 (pbk. : alk. paper)
  1. American Institute of International Law. Declaration of the
Rights and Duties of Nations--Congresses. 2. International law--
Congresses. 3. International law--America--Congresses. 4.
Scott, James Brown, 1866-1943. I. Butler, William Elliott, 1939-
II. American Institute of International Law. Declaration of the
Rights and Duties of Nations. III. Title.

  KZ1287.A46S38 2009
  341--dc22

                               2009046637

Printed in the United States of America on acid-free paper

James Brown Scott and the American Institute of International Law

William E. Butler

During the spring of 1911 the distinguished Chilean international lawyer, Dr. Alejandro Alvarez (1868-1960) made a stopover in Washington D. C. while en route to Europe and called upon James Brown Scott (1866-1943), who at the time had recently assumed his new post as Director of the Division of International Law at the Carnegie Endowment for International Peace. Much of his two days in the United States capital Dr. Alvarez spent in the company of Scott discussing aspects of relations between the United States and Latin America, which at the time had reached a nadir for various reasons.

In a letter dated 3 June 1911 to the President of the Carnegie Endowment, Elihu Root (1845-1937), Scott recounted the essence of the conversations with Alvarez and the initiative that he proposed to take as a result of these meetings.[1] Scott considered that the lamentable state of relations between the United States and the nations of South and Central America would improve "... as a result of an interchange of thought and the creation of a better understanding". If the peoples of the various countries could be brought into closer touch, Scott suggested, "diplomatic relations

---

1. The same letter of the same date was also addressed to the President of Columbia University, Dr. Nicholas Murray Butler. For an account of the letter, of the American Institute of International Law in general, and of Scott's role I rely primarily in this essay upon the unnumbered chapter in the unpublished biography of James Brown Scott prepared by his close friend and associate, George Finch. The manuscript versions (there are several) repose in the James Brown Scott Papers, Box 69, Folder 1, Georgetown University Library, Special Collections Division, Washington D. C.

would take care of themselves". He proposed, *inter alia*, an interchange of thought to be created by "the exchange of professors and students" to draw the nations closer together intellectually.

In order to "set on foot" a movement for the dissemination of those principles of law and justice to regulate the foreign relations of the countries concerned, Scott proposed the "establishment in the capital of each Latin American country of a local society of international law" to work in harmony with the relatively recently founded American Society of International Law (1906).[2] This suggestion found favor with Alvarez. After "… reflection and very much discussion", Alvarez and Scott came to the view that the "best way to draw the leaders of thought together would be to create an American Institute of International Law" in which each country should have equal representation of, say, five members. The members from each country would organize a local society of international law in their respective capital cities. The American Institute of International Law would assemble annually, usually in Washington D. C., to discuss "scientific questions of international law", especially those relating to peace. Gradually a code of international law might be drafted to represent the "enlightened thought" of American publicists.

These principles, as will be evident from this book, carried over for the most part to the American Institute of International Law as formed. The structure represented a rather cunning combination of the organizational forms used by the Institut de droit international

---

2. James Brown Scott reported to the 1914 Business Meeting of the American Society of International Law on the measures underway to form the American Institute of International Law. The meeting "… authorized Elihu Root to take the steps needed to enter into a relationship with this Institute". See F. L.Kirgis, *The American Society of International Law's First Century 1906-2006* (2006), p. 37.

and the American Society of International Law, but their conceptual combination gave the Alvarez/Scott scheme a distinctive configuration. First, the American Institute of International Law and the local societies to be formed in each country (in the United States, the American Society of International Law (ASIL) already existed) were seen as part and parcel of an integral relationship. Second, there seemed to be no illusions that in many, if not most, Latin American nations the societies formed would have only a few members, perhaps in some cases not more than the five who were elected to the American Institute of International Law.

Elihu Root gave his unreserved support to the proposed scheme and subsequently consented to serve as the Honorary President of the Institute.

Alvarez in the meantime proceeded on to Europe, where he spent considerable time in his capacity as the Jurisconsult of the Chilean Ministry of Foreign Affairs, a member of the Permanent Court of Arbitration at The Hague, and, more significantly in this connection, counselor to the Chilean diplomatic missions in Europe. He was still in Paris when Scott arrived to attend the meeting of a committee of the Institut de droit international. On 10 October 1911 Alvarez and Scott collaborated to draft and sign a confidential letter explaining the nature and scope of the proposed American Institute of International Law to colleagues in each of the American republics and inviting their collaboration.[3] Scott and Alvarez also consulted with members of the Institut de droit international either in conversation or in writing to secure support for the project.[4]

---

3. For the text of the Letter, see *American Journal of International Law*, VI (1912), pp. 952-954.
4. Professors A. de Lapradelle and Paul Fauchille were among those lending their support to the proposal in the form of positive articles or letters. These, together with opinions from other friendly sources, were

Minor criticisms were received. Some were concerned that the American Institute would be confused with the Institut de droit international. Alvarez's association with the project led some to assume that it would serve as a vehicle for promoting his conception of an "American international law". Scott replied to these criticisms in identical letters dated 7 November 1912 to the leading members of the Institut de droit international, pointing out that:

> The name "American" has been used for geographical reasons, to distinguish this Institute from the (international) Institute of International Law, of which you are an honored member, not to suggest that there is or can be an American International Law. There are indeed American problems to be solved by the application of the generally recognized principles of international law, and, if these principles do not suffice, it may well be that they will be required to be developed in the future, as in the past, to meet new and changed conditions. I make this statement, in order that there may be no mistake as to our purpose, which is to contribute, to the full extent of our abilities, to the development and the dissemination of a system of international law, as it has been created by the weight and wisdom of European publicists.[5]

Having completed his consultations, Scott then proceeded to organize the American Institute of International Law. He drafted the Constitution (pp.107-112 below) and the By-Laws (pp. 113-120 below), drawing upon the example of the Institut de droit

---

published in the *Revue générale de droit international public*, XIX (1912), i-vii, 329-344, and collected by the American Institute of International Law in *Institut Américain de droit international: historique, notes, opinions* (Washington D. C., 1916). There is no English language version of this volume.

5. Quoted from Finch, note 1 above.

international, and circulated them to the international lawyers first contacted about the project by way of a "Confidential Note" dated 4 July 1912.[6] These recipients were invited to sign and return the documents and thereby become charter members[7] of the American Institute. They were further requested to authorize the proposers to undertake a temporary organization.

Alvarez had by now returned to the western hemisphere to attend the session of the International Commission of Jurists at Rio de Janeiro in July 1912. There he succeeded in obtaining a formal resolution from the Commission commending the initiative taken to establish the American Institute and recording the opinion of a committee of the Rio Commission that the American Institute would be of great value and assistance in the work of codification which the statesmen of the New World had in mind.

Having been authorized by the Latin American recipients of the invitation to proceed, Scott and Alvarez declared the American Institute of International Law to be founded as from 12 October 1912 – Columbus Day. The provisional officers designated became permanent in office. Elihu Root served as Honorary President; James Brown Scott as President; Alejandro Alvarez as Secretary General; Luis Anderson as Treasurer.

---

6. The Note was published in the *American Journal of International Law*, VI (1912), pp. 954-957.

7. There was one charter member from each of twenty-one countries, as follows: Luis M. Drago (Argentina); Alberto Gutierrez (Bolivia); Ruy Barbosa (Brazil); Alejandro Alvarez (Chile); A. J. Uribe (Colombia); Luis Anderson (Costa Rica); A. S. de Bustamante (Cuba); A. J. Montolio (Dominican Republic); R.Arizaga (Ecuador); A. B. Jauregui (Guatemala); J. N. Leger (Haiti); A. Membreno (Honduras); J. D. Casasus (Mexico); S. Castrillo (Nicaragua); F. Boyd (Panama); M. Gondra (Paraguay); R. Ribeyro (Peru); R. S. Lopez (Salvador); J. B. Scott (United States); C. M. de Pena (Uruguay); and J. G. Fortoul (Venezuela).

The superstructure of the American Institute having been created,[8] Scott and Alvarez sent a circular note to the charter members asking that they proceed immediately with the establishment of an international law society in each country in accordance with the Constitution of the American Institute.[9] In a covering letter dated 18 December 1912 Scott and Alvarez explained that the formation of individual country societies was beyond their individual capacities and required collaborative efforts on the part of all associated with the American Institute.

As events were to demonstrate, forming individual international law societies in twenty Latin American countries was also beyond the abilities of the charter members. It required a fortunate combination of political and diplomatic serendipity and astuteness on the part of James Brown Scott to reach this objective. A key factor was the stature of Elihu Root in Latin America. In his capacity as United States Secretary of State he had visited South America and cultivated a sympathetic understanding for that part of the world which proved to be indispensible when, as President of the Carnegie Endowment for International Peace, he sought to enlist interest and cooperation with its program in the southern hemisphere.

The Carnegie Endowment invited Robert Bacon (1860-1919), who had served as Assistant Secretary of State under Mr. Root and later became Secretary of State in his own right, to visit South America on behalf of the Endowment with a view to encouraging cooperation with specific projects in each of the Endowment's three divisions of activity. The formation of national societies of

---

8. Scott summarized the process in his note "The American Institute of International Law", *University of Pennsylvania Law Review*. LXI (1912-13), pp. 580-587.
9. The letter was published in the English and Spanish-language editions of the *American Journal of International Law*, VII (1913), pp. 163-167.

international law to be affiliated with the American Institute of International Law was among the projects. Bacon accepted the assignment while on his way home from the Orient and determined to leave for Latin America from Lisbon. Scott and Alvarez met him in Paris to brief him about the American Institute of International Law and the various national societies.[10] Scott even wrote some of the speeches which Bacon would deliver.

Advance preparations and thorough briefings ensured a cordial reception at the highest levels of government in all the countries which he visited. The Presidents of Brazil, Uruguay, Chile, and Peru received him personally, and he met with senior ministers throughout his journey. In each of the capitals which he visited, committees were organized to form a national society of international law.

The Second Pan American Scientific Congress held at Washington D. C. in December 1915 provided the occasion for the formal launching of the American Institute of International Law. Scott circulated this suggestion to the charter members of the American Institute and the organizing committees on 25 August 1914, urging that all necessary organizational measures be completed and members be nominated for election as Titular Members of the Institute. Here too philanthropy and diplomacy were in happy combination, for the letters were delivered by diplomatic pouch to the American missions in each country for forwarding on to the individuals concerned.

The outbreak of the First World War was a source of discouragement for those who believed in the importance of international law. The Institut de droit international discontinued its sessions, not least because its membership was divided between

10. On Bacon's instructions and his report of the visit, see *For Better Relations with Our Latin American Neighbors* (Washington D. C., 1916).

friends and foes. In Latin America the organization of national societies of international law was adversely affected, as one would expect, but the need for their existence was imperative given the structure of the American Institute. While the American Institute shared common aims with its European counterpart, its membership depended upon national societies in each country recommending candidates for full membership. Until such societies had been created and submitted nominations for Titular Members, the American Institute could not function properly.

On 22 February 1915 Scott and Alvarez circulated a lengthy letter to the charter members setting out what had been accomplished to date and what remained to be done before the American Institute could operate at full strength: "Today, when European civilization is passing through a formidable crisis, Latin America must organize in order to become the spokesman of law and justice in international relations".[11] While this appeal produced some results, ultimately the Carnegie Endowment was able to provide travel subventions for many of those invited to the Second Pan American Scientific Congress, supporting as its guests three delegates from each Latin American government to be chosen by the States concerned provided that at least one international lawyer was included among the three. These invitations were likewise communicated through diplomatic channels, and it was intimated that in choosing their international lawyer, the charter member or other equally distinguished member of the respective national society of international law would be especially welcomed.

As these arrangements were being pursued, Robert Lansing (1864-1928) was appointed to become the United States Secretary of State. One of the founders of the American Society of

---

11. For the full text of the letter, see *Yearbook of the Carnegie Endowment* (1915), pp. 121-130.

International Law and a member from the United States of the American Institute of International Law, Lansing was sympathetic to "manifesting the interest of the Department of State in the successful formation of national societies of international law and the creation of the American Institute".[12] The official program of the Second Pan American Scientific Congress distributed to the ministers of foreign affairs of all the American republics included the following passages:

> It is hoped that the American Institute of International Law, which is composed of representatives of the different national societies in the Pan American countries, may be formally inaugurated and hold its first session in Washington, under the auspices of the Second Pan American Scientific Congress.
>
> National societies have been formed in Brazil, Chile, Mexico, Nicaragua, Peru, and Uruguay, and are in process of formation in others. It is believed that in this way international law, consisting not merely of the rights but of the duties of nations, will be brought home to the peoples of the different countries through the national societies composed of persons interested in the subject, versed in its principles, and competent to expound and to popularize them.
>
> The Institute, composed of five publicists from each American country, recommended by the national societies, will, it is hoped, do for international law in the Americas what the older Institute of International Law has done for international law in general, and the scientific co-operation of American publicists will not only advance the cause of international law and base the actions of governments upon its principles, but will strengthen the bonds of sympathy which exist between and among the American republics.

---

12. See Finch, note 1 above.

The formation of these societies in all of the countries of Central and South America will materially aid in this educational process, and any encouragement or co-operation which the Governments of the American Republics can extend will give the movement an official impetus.

Scott circulated reminders of the same character on 7 April 1915 through the heads of United States embassies and legations accredited to the South and Central American countries to the respective ministries of foreign affairs, members of the organizing committees, and charter members of the American Institute. Enclosed with these reminders was a Decree of the President of Uruguay, dated 29 December 1914, appointing the committee to organize a national society of international law and declaring that such society in Uruguay would have the legal status of an institution of public interest.

This campaign ultimately produced results. A number of countries emulated the Uruguayan decree and in others the minister of foreign affairs took the initiative directly. Lansing used his personal influence in several capitals through diplomatic channels. The formation of a national society occurred in each American republic in time for participation in the Second Pan American Scientific Congress on 27 December 1915. The Governing Board of the Pan American Union had, in a resolution adopted 1 December 1915, commended the formation of the American Institute of International Law as a "… step of the highest importance in the moral advancement of the continent and in the strengthening of the sentiments of friendship and harmony among the republics".

Having now completed all the formalities necessary for a fully-fledged existence, the American Institute of International Law met for the first time during the afternoon of 29 December 1915 in the building of the Pan American Union in Washington D. C., a gift from Andrew Carnegie as a Temple of Peace to the American republics. All the meetings of the Institute were integrated into the program of the Section on International Law of the Congress and the annual meeting of the American Society of International Law, which had been deferred from the preceding April in order to accommodate a joint session with these two organizations.

Four members of the American Society of International Law attended the sessions of the American Institute of International Law: Robert Lansing, who in his capacity as Secretary of State welcomed the American Institute on behalf of the United States Government; Elihu Root, as Honorary President of the American Institute; James Brown Scott, as President of the American Institute; and Robert Bacon, whose tour of Latin America had so assisted the creation of the American Institute. Three members were present from the national societies of international law in Haiti and Honduras; two members from societies in Argentina, Bolivia, Brazil, Chile, Ecuador, Guatemala, Peru, and Uruguay; and one each from societies in Colombia, Costa Rica, Cuba, Dominican Republic, El Salvador, Mexico, Nicaragua, Panama, Paraguay, and Venezuela. One of the Chilean delegates also served as the President of the Scientific Congress.

The formal adoption of the Constitution and By-Laws of the American Institute took place at a preliminary meeting presided over by James Brown Scott. The officers of the American Institute selected provisionally were now confirmed in office, and the full quota of members were elected as Titular Members of the American Institute from each of the national societies (for the full List, see the Appendix below, pp. 121-125).

The various remarks made by the President of the American Institute, James Brown Scott, comprise the greater part of this volume. In addition, a number of proposals were submitted to the Institute, including a memorandum from Robert Lansing which recommended that a study be undertaken of the rights and duties of neutrals.[13] Scott himself had prepared, in anticipation of the American Institute being successfully launched, a memorandum proposing that a series of studies be undertaken, among them the preamble from the 1776 Declaration of Independence of the United States of America. The Preamble, he suggested, formulated the "... American conception of the origin, nature, and purpose of the State and as to the function of the Government established within each State". He proposed a study to determine to what extent and in what form the principles of the United States Declaration may be applicable to the States as an artificial person. If his conception commended itself to the American Institute, he said, "we could begin to develop an American international law, based upon an American conception of the State and an American conception of the government thereof".[14]

Scott's proposal was the foundation for the principal outcome of the American Institute's inaugural meeting. On 6 January 1916 the Declaration of the Rights and Duties of Nations was adopted, being based upon Scott's original proposal. The text is reprinted below (pp. 87-88).[15]

---

13. The Memorandum is published in the *Carnegie Endowment Year Book* (1916), p. 127.
14. See Finch, note 1 above, quoting Scott manuscripts not traced.
15. Also see J. B. Scott, "The American Institute of International Law", *American Journal of International Law*, X (1916), pp. 124-126.

Activities and Fate of American Institute of International Law

The American Institute of International Law convened at irregular intervals throughout the interwar era until 1938. Various recommendations were adopted concerning international organizations, and thirty draft projects on international law topics were proposed for its consideration.[16] The Pan American Union, to which the draft projects were submitted, placed 27 of them before the International Commission of American Jurists for the Codification of International Law in April 1927. No less than thirteen of the drafts were incorporated in some manner into the codifications produced by the Commission. Among the subjects were statehood, aliens, law of treaties, diplomatic and consular agents, neutrality at sea, asylum, duties of States in the event of civil war, and the peaceful settlement of disputes.[17]

The first meeting following the inaugural session in Washington D. C. was held, upon the invitation of the Government of Cuba, in the city of Havana from 22 to 27 January 1917 under the aegis of the Cuban Society of International Law. Recommendations adopted on this occasion called for periodic meetings of the Hague conferences and the ratification of and compliance with the Hague conventions, official acceptance of the principles of law contained in the Declaration of the Rights and Duties of Nations endorsed in January 1916 in Washington D. C.[18] Peaceful settlement of disputes

---

16. On the draft projects, see *American Journal of International Law*, XX (1926), pp. 300-384 (Special Supplement).
17. See J. B. Scott, "The Gradual and Progressive Codification of International Law", *American Journal of International Law*, XXI (1927), p. 417.
18. See *The Recommendations of Habana Concerning International Organization Adopted by the American Institute of International Law, January 23, 1917* (1917).

was of major interest at this meeting, including good offices, conciliation, mediation, arbitration, and judicial adjudication.[19]

All the considerable interest in pacific settlement of disputes, however, was not sufficient to rescue from abolition the first permanent international court to be established on this planet – the Central American Court of Justice created by the Central American Peace Conference held at Washington D. C. in 1907 under the chairmanship of Elihu Root, then the United States Secretary of State. Andrew Carnegie was in attendance at the Conference and later donated funds for the court house of the Court of Justice to be built at San José, Costa Rica (when the building was destroyed by earthquake a few years later, Carnegie duplicated his gift to rebuild it). On 30 September 1916 the Central American Court of Justice actually rendered a decision determining that a Treaty of 5 August 1914 between the United States and Nicaragua to build an inter-oceanic canal violated the territorial rights of Costa Rica and neighboring States. Although Nicaragua refused to accept the decision, the United States was prepared to accept it and settle the dispute diplomatically. At the Havana meeting the American Institute of International Law adopted a recommendation to continue the existence of the Court, due to disappear unless the ten-year period for which it was created would be extended. The treaty was not renewed, notwithstanding the appeal of the American Institute of International Law sent on 1 March 1918. The appeal was ignored

---

19. The American Institute published the proceedings of the Havana meeting in French and Spanish language versions. See *Acta Final de la Sesion de la Habana* (Havana, 1917). They were even approved by and incorporated in the platform of the Republican Party of the State of New York at its convention held on 20 February 1920. See the *New York Times*, 21 February 1920.

and the Court went out of existence on 17 March 1918 when its ten-year term lapsed.[20]

A perhaps unexpected ancillary outcome of the turn towards Central and South America on the part of the United States international legal community was the appearance of a Spanish-language edition of the *American Journal of International Law*. Through the intervention of James Brown Scott acting in his capacity as Director of the Division of International Law of the Carnegie Endowment for International Peace, the Board of Trustees approved a recommendation to appropriate a portion of the revenues of the Endowment to strengthen and increase the usefulness of journals of international law. The American Society of International law was among those chosen for support, and commencing with the issue of January 1912 its journal was distributed in a Spanish-language version throughout Mexico and Central and South America. The Proceedings of the Society were included in the scheme.[21] Support continued through 1921, when publication of the translated edition was terminated.

Once the American Institute of International Law was in operation, it was decided a Spanish-language journal should serve as the organ of the Institute and an offer from Dr. Antoni S. de Bustamante (1865-1951) to edit such a journal was accepted. The Carnegie Endowment transferred limited financial support to his *Revista Americana de derecho internacional*, which commenced publication as a quarterly in 1922 and survived throughout the interwar period, albeit with personal subsidies from the editor.

A disinterested assessment of the contributions of the American Institute of International Law has yet to be undertaken. An

---

20. See the *Carnegie Endowment Year Book* (1918), pp. 118-120.
21. See "The Spanish Edition of the American Journal of International Law", *American Journal of International Law*, VI (1912), pp. 957-959.

appreciative account of its early activities may be found in an early dissertation.[22] The activities of the Institute in its declining years were summarized usefully in a Cuban publication.[23] The American Institute of International Law was among the private institutions designated by the Advisory Committee of Jurists at The Hague to share in preparatory labors for a new Hague Conference, although the project never came to fruition.

Greater impetus in the direction of codification came thanks to the initiative of Charles Evan Hughes (1862-1948), the United States Secretary of State and *ex officio* Chairman of the Governing Board of the Pan American Union. On 2 January 1924 the Governing Board of the Pan American Union requested the American Institute to prepare a series of projects on international law to be laid before the International Commission of Jurists at Rio de Janeiro. These led to a number of drafts being generated, the most famous and enduring of which was the Bustamante Code of Private International Law, adopted by fifteen Latin American countries in 1928.

The leadership of the American Institute of International Law determined in 1929 that, if possible, the headquarters of the Institute should be permanently established in Havana, Cuba. The President of Cuba was persuaded to support this suggestion, and on 8 March 1929 issued a decree authorizing the erection of a Palace of the American Institute of International Law as "the contribution of the Republic of Cuba to the very excellent work which the American Institute of International Law is realizing on behalf of inter-American

---

22. S. Cirkovic, *Le droit international nouveau: L'Institut americain de droit internationalson role et son oeuvre*. Preface by N. Politis (Paris, 1926).
23. See *Epitome de las actividades de la institucion, de 1938 a 1942* (Havana, 1943).

culture and peace, and in just response to the honor which this body concedes to the City of Habana, by establishing therein the center of its activities". The Palace was to contain permanent quarters for the Executive Council of the Institute and its Secretariat, and an American Academy of International Law analogous to that in operation at The Hague.[24] Although the cornerstone was ceremoniously laid in May 1929, the edifice was never completed "due to subsequent economic and political complications in Cuba ...".[25]

Efforts of the United States to promote women's rights during the early 1930s through the Pan American Union created disenchantment with the American Institute of International Law: "The bitter struggle at the Montevideo Conference [3-26 December 1933] over the proposals of the National Women's Party of the United States sponsored by the American Institute produced outspoken dissatisfaction and resulted in the adoption of a long detailed resolution in regard to future procedures for the codification of international law at inter-American Conferences".[26] The resolution effectively discontinued the function of the American Institute as an adviser to the Pan American Union previously bestowed upon the Institute. "Thus, when the Institute attempted at Montevideo to include political and local aspects regarding women's rights along with its juridical projects of a theoretical and

---

24. The decree was gazette in the *Gaceta Oficial*, 12 March 1929; an English translation appeared in the *Carnegie Endowment Year Book* (1929), pp. 197-198.
25. Finch, note 1 above. For a description of the planned building, see Secretary of Public Works, *Proyecto descriptivo del estudio preliminar del palacio del Instituto Americano de derecho internacional* [Havana, 1929].
26. Finch, note 1 above.

universal nature, it lost its official standing before the Inter-American Conferences".[27] Dr. Alvarez, who was present at Montevideo, reported in a Letter dated 22 December 1933 to James Brown Scott sent from on board the steamer after he had departed that certain leading delegates had "revealed themselves as mortal enemies of the Institute and 'declared that it was a dead organization'". One result of the conflict was that the Carnegie Endowment withdrew financial support from the American Institute completely.

For several years the American Institute remained, as Scott put it in one of his Reports to the Carnegie Endowment, "in abeyance". A promising renaissance originated with the formation of the Section of International and Comparative Law within the American Bar Association in 1937. That Section recommended that the American Institute of International Law resume its regular activities and take advantage of the forthcoming Eighth International Conference of American States at Lima, Peru, in 1938 to hold a formal session. The Peruvian Government issued an invitation to do so, and 21 out of a possible 24 members succeeded in being present. Vacancies in membership were filled and measures introduced to reduce the dependence upon national societies in each country. However, the Conference did not reinstate the American Institute as part of the revised codification machinery which it endorsed on the occasion. Throughout the remaining years of its existence, the American Institute engaged in codification exercises of a purely private nature.

From time to time thereafter officers of the American Institute met to discuss future activities and hear reports. In 1941-42 there were several informal meetings in Washington D. C. to discuss strengthening the Institute. All these activities ceased with the death

---

27. Finch, note 1 above.

of James Brown Scott on 25 June 1943. The vacancy in the presidency of the Institute occasioned by his death was never filled.

The Book

The present volume is one of several generated by the original proposal and campaign to create the American Institute of International Law. It reproduces and/or references the principal documents leading to the creation of the Institute. A French language version appeared at more or less the same time.[28] The United States Government issued a substantial volume on the Pan American Conference,[29] and the Carnegie Endowment followed with a pamphlet concerning the recommendations on international law adopted at the Congress.[30]

The Author

James Brown Scott was born near Kincardine, Canada, on 3 June 1866, the youngest child of John Scott (1830-1885) and Jeannette Brown (1831-1901). His father was a stone cutter, and

---

28. Scott, *Institut Américain de droit international: Sa Déclaration des droits et devoirs des nations* (1916).
29. See Scott, *The Final Act and Interpretive Commentary Thereon* ... (1916). "The volume contains, in addition, the program as finally carried out, the list of scientific institutions associations, learned societies participating in the Congress, and the lists of names of all persons invited to take part in the proceedings".
30. See Scott (ed.), *Recommendations on International Law and Official Commentary Thereon of the Sceond Pan American Scientific Congress: held in Washington, December 27, 1915-January 8, 1916* (1916).

his mother the daughter of a weaver. Both had emigrated in 1849 from Scotland to New York, where they met and married in 1853 before moving to Canada. There were four other children in the family, three girls and a boy: Mary, Margaret, John, and Jeannette. John died in childhood, aged 15. Three years after the birth of James, the family left Canada for Philadelphia, returned to Canada in 1871, and relocated permanently to Philadelphia in 1876.

James and his sisters were provided with a good education. When their father passed away they were left with sufficient funds to complete their studies until they became self-supporting. All the Scott children excelled in their schooling and completed their education in Europe. Mary, the eldest, studied in Berlin, Vienna, and Munich after graduating from the Women's Medical College in Philadelphia; she was among the first women to be admitted to the Institut Pasteur (Paris). Upon her return to the United States, she became a specialist in children's diseases, an interest aroused by the boyhood death of her brother John.

Margaret became a professor of romance languages upon completing her studies in France and Germany at initially the University of Illinois and then Syracuse University. She outlived the other members of the family.

Jeannette, the youngest sister, studied art and followed the career of a painter. Upon graduation from the School of Design in Philadelphia, she attended the Pennsylvania Academy of Fine Arts and then studied in Europe for five years, from 1889 to 1894. Returning to the United States, she accepted a position as instructor in painting at Syracuse University, retiring in 1927 as head of the Department of Painting with the degree of Doctor of Fine Arts.[31]

31. Drawn from the unpublished biography of James Brown Scott by George Finch, in the James Brown Scott Papers, Box 69, Folder 1, Georgetown University Library, Special Collections Division, Washington D. C.

She was interested in women's rights and helped to finance the Inter American Commission of Women, created by the Sixth Pan American Conference (Havana, 1928), the first juridical Commission of Women ever established by governments acting in concert.

James Brown Scott completed his secondary schooling in Philadelphia and was admitted to Harvard College and graduated *summa cum laude* in 1890 with his B.A., staying on a further year to complete his A. M. (1891).[32] His career as an international lawyer commenced with his being selected for a Parker Fellowship at Harvard which he held for three years. He did not attend law school, but instead spent a year at Heidelberg University, where he was awarded the *juris utriusque doctor*. Upon returning to the United States, he pursued the practice of law in California. He was not distracted from academic legal life for long. In 1896 he organized the Law School at Los Angeles (now the University of Southern California School of Law) and was then enticed to become the Dean of the University of Illinois Law School (1899-1903). The Columbia Law School persuaded him to come to New York (1903-06),[33] and he might have remained there had he not written

---

32. For biographical materials on Scott, I have had the benefit of the James Brown Scott Papers held at Georgetown University, which contain the manuscript biography by George Finch and numerous curriculum vitas prepared by Scott himself for various occasions. Among printed materials, see obituaries in the *American Journal of International Law*, XXXVII (1943), 508 (G. A. Finch); XXXVII (1943), 559-561 (F. R. Coudert); XXXVIII (1944), 183-217 (G. A. Finch); *Transactions of the Grotius Society*, XXIX (1943), vii-viii (Cecil J. B. Hurst); and D. Stevens, *Paintings & Drawings of Jeannette Scott 1864-1937* (1940).

33. While at Columbia he produced J. B. Scott (ed.), *Cases on Quasi-Contracts* (1905) and the following year, having removed to George Washington University, Scott (ed.), *Cases on Equity Jurisdiction* (1906), in two volumes; and Scott (ed.), *Cases on International Law, Selected*

a letter to the United States Secretary of State suggesting that a legal advisor might be appointed to the Department and that he might be considered a candidate for the position.

His interview made an excellent impression, and he moved to the nation's capital, where he remained until 1940, when he retired to his summer home in nearby Annapolis. He married Adele Cooper Scott in 1901.

During the years 1905-06 he was actively involved with others in forming the American Society of International Law.[34] From 1895 to 1914 members of what many regard as the United States "foreign policy establishment" assembled each year at Lake Mohonk in upstate New York to discuss the preservation of peace and, more particularly, the perceived importance of international arbitration as an alternative to war. James Brown Scott was present at the eleventh conference from 31 May to 2 June 1905, where the American Society of International Law was conceived. He acted as one of an informal committee of three[35] which decided to put the proposal for the Society to those in attendance at the Conference and then as the secretary of the meeting of twenty-four Conference participants who supported the proposal unanimously and appointed a committee of seven to draft a constitution for the Society. When the Society constitution was ultimately adopted, Scott was appointed Recording Secretary and a member of the Executive Council of

---

from Decisions of English and American Courts (1902), revised and published in 1906 by West Publishing Co., and revised throughout the interwar period.

34. See F. L. Kirgis, *The American Society of International Law's First Century 1906-2006* [(2006)].

35. The other two members being Robert Lansing, later the United States Secretary of State, and Professor G. W. Kirchwey, sometime President of the American Peace Society.

the Society. An integral part of the scheme to organize the Society was the establishment of a journal, and at the twelfth meeting at Lake Mohonk on 1 June 1906 the Executive Council appointed Scott as Managing Editor of the *American Journal of International Law*. The journal has appeared quarterly thereafter; Scott advanced from his own pocket the funds necessary to print the first two issues, being later reimbursed.

While acting as the Solicitor for the Department of State, he took a dual appointment at the George Washington University Law School (1906-11) and also lectured at The Johns Hopkins University (1906-16). After service during the First World War and involvement in the negotiations of the postwar settlements, he accepted appointment to the School of Foreign Service at Georgetown University from 1921 until his retirement. He acted as an exchange professor at various times at the Universities of Chile, Havana, Montevideo, Salamanca, Berlin, Frankfurt, Göttingen, Kiel, and Munich, among others.

He received seventeen honorary degrees: (Syracuse, Salamanca, Paris (Sorbonne), Universidad Mayor de San Marcos (Peru), George Washington, St. John's College (Annapolis), University of Chile, Warsaw University, University of Habana, Cambridge University, Michigan, Oberlin, Lyon, Queen's University (Ontario), Athens, Georgetown, and Southern California).

Elected an Associate of the Institut de droit international in 1908, he became a full member in 1910 and eventually served as President. He was elected to the Royal Academy of Sciences in Belgium (1919), to the Institut de France (1921), to the American Academy of Arts and Sciences (1935), among a number of distinctions of this kind. A number of countries (Belgium, Yugoslavia, Serbia, Chile, Italy, Ecuador, Romania, Netherlands, and Cuba included) conferred decorations upon him.

Having persuaded the Carnegie Institution to support his Project on the classics of international law, he accepted appointment as secretary of what became the Carnegie Endowment for International Peace and director of the Division of International Law. In both capacities for more than three decades, to borrow the apt phrase of Manley Ottmer Hudson (1886-1956), he "... fathered and fostered the development of international law during the greatest period of its history".[36]

Sixteenth-century Catholic doctrinal writings continued to constitute a significant portion of his scholarly writings. Not long after receiving his honorary degree from Salamanca University, he initiated measures to arrange a celebration of the 400th anniversary of Vitoria's lectures at the University, dated by common consent to 1532. In 1930 he was awarded a gold and silver plaque for his original research in "establishing the title of Francisco de Vittoria ... a Dominican priest, as the founder of modern International Law".[37]

At a luncheon of the members of the Institut de droit international in 1932 it was decided to form the International Association of Francis of Vitoria and of Suarez.[38] The 30 or so members present were regarded as charter members, with a ceiling on membership of 100 and local societies to be formed in nations

---

36. See the Remarks of Manley O. Hudson, in "Portrait of Dr. James Brown Scott", *Harvard Alumni Bulletin*, XXXIII, no. 14 (1 January 1931), p. 419.

37. Press Release, dated 5 April 1930, James Brown Scott Papers, Box 63, Folder 8, Georgetown University Library, Special Collections Division, Washington D. C.

38. In effect this was to be an international "umbrella" association for national societies such as the Asociacion Francisco de Vitoria, established in 1928 as related by James Brown Scott, "Asociacion Francisco de Vitoria", *American Journal of International Law*, XXII (1928), 136-139. It was the same pattern he used when creating the American Institute of International Law.

accepting and abiding by the principle of international law in their mutual relations. No country could have more than ten members on the international body. Dr. Nicolas Politis (1872-1942) was elected the President and Dr. Alfred Verdross (1890-19?), the Secretary-General. The Statutes of the International Association Vitoria-Suarez were approved by the Constitutive General Assembly at Oslo on 17 August 1932 (the Association actually operating within the framework of meetings of the Institut de droit international). James Brown Scott was elected First Vice President of the Association in 1936 and recruited a number of his close professional colleagues to be elected among the maximum quota of ten in the International Association. Members of the international association were active throughout the 1930s in propagating the doctrines of Vitoria, and the association itself identified with a number of publications.[39]

Diplomacy played an important role in his career. In 1907 he was a technical delegate to the Second Hague Peace Conference. From 1914 to 1917 he was the Chairman of the United States Neutrality Board, and in 1919 acted as the legal adviser to the delegation of the United States at the Paris Peace Conference. During 1922-23 he was the legal adviser to the American delegates at the Washington Conference on the Limitation of Armaments. In 1927 he was a member of the Inter-American Commission of Jurists which met at Rio de Janeiro. The following year he served as delegate to the Sixth International Conference of American States at Havana.

---

39. Among them *Vitoria et Suarez: contribution des théologiens au droit international moderne*, Preface by James Brown Scott (1939).

The Chichele Chair of International Law

Upon the retirement of Professor Sir Thomas Erskine Holland (1835-1926), the Chichele Chair of International Law became vacant at Oxford University in 1910. To the surprise of many, James Brown Scott decided to make application for the position. The application itself is a remarkable document – a printed booklet of considerable length setting out Dr. Scott's credentials and containing testimonials of his qualifications and character from leading figures throughout Europe and the United States.

The Scott Papers do not disclose whether Erskine persuaded or encouraged Scott to apply for the position or not.[40] The electors took a considerable time to come to a view on who should be appointed, perhaps because they were divided. Scott was kept in contact with what was happening by Professor Lassa Oppenheim (1858-1919), who held the Whewell Chair at Cambridge University. On 22 November 1910 Oppenheim wrote from Whewell House in Cambridge:

> … As regards the Oxford chair, I have heard nothing which would indicate how matters are going on. Everybody knows that you are Holland's candidate, and people who discuss you may be divided into two camps, although everybody agrees that you are the best candidate. To the one camp belong Pollock [Sir Frederick Pollock (1845-1937) – WEB], Whittuck [Edward Arthur Whittuck (1844-1924)] – WEB], and others, with a wide horizon, who say that the best man ought to have it no matter whether he be an English subject or not. To the other camp belong a number

---

40. Scott had persuaded Erskine to edit the works of Richard Zouche (1590-1661) for the Classics of International Law series. The volumes appeared in 1911. On Erskine's tenure in the Chair, see T. E. Erskine, *A Valedictory Retrospect (1874-1910)* (1910).

of small minded people who say that to appoint an American would be awkward in view of the possibility of an Anglo-American conflict. Since the more influential people belong to the first mentioned class I trust that your election is certain. But so much is absolutely certain that if you fail to be elected the only matter which bared [sic] your election is that you are not an English subject. I shall send a wire anyhow as soon as I hear of the result.

On 16 December 1910 Oppenheim wrote:[41]

... I suppose that Holland provides you with news in this matter. I hear very little, but the following may be of interest: I hear from a good source that the President of the Admiralty Court who is one of the electors stands firm for Macdonnell [Sir John Macdonnell (1846-1921 – WEB]. Westlake [John Westlake (1828-1913) – WEB] works hard – so Whittuck writes me – for Higgins [Alexander Pearce Higgins (1865-1935) – WEB]. There is also a rumour that Fromageot is supported by one of the electors. Another rumour is that the election is postponed on account of the political crisis, and there is also a rumour that the postponement is due to the fact that the electors have not yet come to an agreement ...

It was perhaps the example of Professor Oppenheim which Scott followed in developing his application for the Chair. Oppenheim supplied Scott with a copy of his own application for the Whewell Chair, printed by the University Press Cambridge and dated 6 July 1908.

Scott was not elected to the Chair, impressive as his credentials were.

_____

41. Both letters are in the James Brown Scott Papers Box 57, Folder 12, Georgetown University Library, Special Collections Division, Washington D. C.

American Society for Judicial Settlement of International Disputes

Scott's unflagging efforts in support of the establishment of an international court of justice were pursued partly through diplomatic channels and partly through the generation of popular public support in favor of such an institution. To the latter end he played the key part in creating the American Society for Judicial Settlement of International Disputes, of which he was elected the first president. The first international conference of the Society was held at Washington D. C. on 15-17 December 1910 and attended principally by businessmen, educators, diplomats, and federal and state legislators.

The reference to "judicial" settlement was narrowly understood; arbitration was not included, as Scott made clear in his opening remarks to the constitutive conference: The purposes of the Society are "... limited to a discussion of the judicial determination, as distinguished from the arbitral adjustment, of international controversies. It seeks to strengthen sentiment where existing, and to create sentiment where it does not exist, in favor of judicial settlement. It stands for a permanent court, as distinguished from a temporary tribunal ... It stands for judicial decision according to principles of law, not compromise according to the standards of diplomacy ... We are not opposed to arbitration. On the contrary, we favor it individually, but arbitration as such falls beyond the scope of our labors".[42]

There were six conferences of the American Society in all, the last in 1916. They greatly informed efforts following the First World War to create the Permanent Court of International Justice.

---

42. *Proceedings of the Conference on the Judicial Settlement of International Disputes* (1910), p. 3.

Court of Arbitral Justice

James Brown Scott's energies in support of the judicial settlement of disputes as the exclusive concern of the American Society for the Judicial Settlement of International Disputes reflected no disenchantment with arbitration as an alternative method of dispute resolution – to use a term in fashion today but not at the time. Having been appointed as technical expert of the United States to the Second Hague Peace Conference of 1907 after merely a year or so of service as Solicitor for the Department of State, Scott took "… a conspicuous, one may even say the leading part, in preparing and urging the adoption of the draft for a convention for a Court of Arbitral Justice, and was extremely active and useful in promoting all the conventions adopted by the Conference".[43]

Scott was selected by the Second Hague Peace Conference to prepare the official report to the Conference in respect of the draft Convention for the Establishment of a Court of Arbitral Justice. It was he who explained to the Conference what the draft intended, article by article, and urged its adoption with great eloquence. Although in the end the Conference merely recommended the draft convention to the signatory powers rather then adopting the text itself, it was felt that considerable progress had been made in the right direction. At the Naval Conference in London during 1908-09, which was to agree the law to be applied by a proposed International Prize Court, Scott urged that the United States propose the International Prize Court be vested with the jurisdiction and functions of the Court of Arbitral Justice and, when sitting, should be guided by the draft convention for the establishment of the Arbitral Court. The proposal was made, but for sundry reasons which culminated in the refusal of the United Kingdom to ratify the

---

43. Letter of David Jayne Hill, 18 January 1917, quoted in note 27 below, p. 18.

Prize Court Convention, the Court of Arbitral Justice never came into being. The United States did ratify, but that action did not move the United Kingdom to like action. The proposal ultimately came to an end. Scott persisted with initiatives to revive the scheme in some way. These were ultimately overtaken by the outbreak of the First World War.

The Nobel Peace Prize

James Brown Scott was nominated on at least six occasions for the Nobel Peace Prize, although never with success. The first and most concerted effort on his behalf was undertaken in late 1916 for presumably the Prize awarded in 1917. A substantial printed Memorial, dated 29 December 1916, was submitted on his behalf.[44]

A junior Norwegian diplomat and great admirer of Scott, Gregers W. Gram, informed Scott on 2 January 1923 that he had twice proposed him for the Nobel Prize and intended to do so a third time.[45]

On 13 February 1927 the eminent French international lawyer, Gilbert Gidel (1880-1958), wrote Scott to say: "I believe that no one other than you deserves the Nobel Peace Prize and I shall take advantage of my right of nomination to put forward your candidacy".[46]

---

44. See *Memorial in Support of the Nomination of James Brown Scott for the Nobel Peace Prize* [n.p., 1917]. [iv], 71 p. Copies are held in the James Brown Scott Papers, Box 59, Folder 5, Georgetown Univesity Library, Special Collections Division, Washington D. C.
45. James Brown Scott Papers, Box 59, Folder 6.
46. James Brown Scott Paper, Box 59, Folder 6: "j'ai estime que nul plus que vous n'etait digne du Prix Nobel de la Paix et j'ai profite de mon droit de presentation pour poser votre candidature".

Professor Karl Strupp (1886-1940) wrote to Scott on New Year's Day of 1937 informing him of his nomination:[47]

> Permit me to say that I have proposed you, the father of the Permanent Court of International Justice, for the Nobel Prize; and may I dedicate to you, in the same capacity, my Commentary on the Status and Reglement of this court, which I hope to finish by the end of 1937?

Other Publications

James Brown Scott awaits his proper bibliographer. He published extensively (one would imagine well over 1,000 books, articles, reviews, and translations),[48] but both the volume and nature of his publications were skewed by his association with the Carnegie Institution and later the Carnegie Endowment for International Peace and as the principal moving force behind the *American Journal of International Law*. From 1907 to 1916 inclusive Scott published 266 editorial comments, mostly concerned with topics bearing upon international relations from the standpoint of an international lawyer dedicated to international peace, fourteen leading articles, and 58 book reviews. The series of volumes published as "Classics of International Law", all under his general editorship and many containing a learned introduction by his hand, came to twenty-two titles in forty volumes. A "spin-off" of this project was a two-volume work: Scott (ed.), *The Armed Neutralities*

---

47. James Brown Scott Papers, Box 59, Folder 6. Strupp wrote in German; Scott had the letter translated, and I have quoted the translation supplied to him.
48. The Harvard Law School Library records more than 200 books and pamphlets under his name.

of 1780 and 1800: A Collection of Official Documents Preceded by the Views of Representative Publicists (1918).

He was a popular lecturer frequently invited throughout the country and Europe to deliver not merely single addresses but an entire *cours* dedicated to a particular subject, such as the Hague peace conferences,[49] or dispute settlement. Many found their way into print as monographs or special issues of student law reviews. A number were translated into Spanish or French, usually under Carnegie Endowment auspices.

A considerable portion of his larger works comprised edited, translated, and thoroughly annotated collections of documents which in his day could not have been commercially published without Carnegie Endowment support. All without exception have retained their value for legal scholarship, as their frequent reprinting by commercial publishers demonstrates. Among the titles, usually self-explanatory if not brief, are: Scott (ed. & intro.), *Texts of the Peace Conferences at the Hague, 1899 and 1907 with English Translation and Appendix of Related Documents* (1908); Scott (ed. & intro.), *Instructions to the American Delegates to the Hague Peace Conferences and Their Official Reports* (1916); Scott (ed. & intro.), *The Hague Court Reports Comprising the Awards, Accompanied by Syllabi, the Agreements for Arbitration, and Other Documents in Each Case Submitted to the Permanent Court of Arbitration and to Commissions of Inquiry Under the Provisions of the Conventions of 1899 and 1907 for the Pacific Settlement of International Disputes* (1916-1932) in two series; Scott, *The Status of the International Court*

---

49. See Scott, *The Hague Peace Conferences of 1899 and 1907: A Series of Lectures Delivered Before the Johns Hopkins University in the Year 1908* (1909); Scott, *The Judicial Settlement of International Disputes: Addresses at the Geneva Institute of International Relations August 16th and 17th, 1926* (1927).

of Justice with an Appendix of Addresses and Official Documents (1916); Scott (collected & ed.), *Judicial Settlement of Controversies Between States of the American Union: Cases Decided in the Supreme Court of the United States* (1918). 3 vols.; Scott, *James Madison's Notes of Debates in the Federal Convention of 1787 and Their Relation to a More Perfect Society of Nations* (1918); Scott (ed.), *The Declaration of London February 26, 1909: A Collection of Official Papers and Documents Relating to the International Naval Conference Held in London December, 1908 – February, 1909* (1919); Scott, *The United States of America: A Study in International Organization* (1920); Scott, *Observations on Nationality with Especial Reference to the Hague Convention of April 12th, 1930: A Plea for a Single and Impersonal Standard of Nationality in the Law and Practice of Nations* (1931).

With particular reference to the western hemisphere he prepared: Scott, *The American Institute of International Law: Its Declaration of the Rights and Duties of Nations* (1916); Scott (ed. & intro.), *The International Conference of American States 1889-1926: A Collection of the Conventions, Recommendations, Resolutions, Reports, and Motions adopted by the First Six International Conferences of the American States, and Documents relating to the Organization of the Conferences* (1931).

His casebooks, alluded to above, dominated the teaching of international law in the United States for nearly four decades. The first edition of 1902 was succeeded by another in 1906 (with a change of publisher) and contributed to his serving for a number of years as one of the general editors of a casebook series for West Publishing Co. in St. Paul Minnesota. The last edition appeared in 1937 in collaboration with Walter H. E. Jaeger, then Professor of Law and Director of Graduate Research at Georgetown University as the junior author.

Scott's final major work of this genre appeared in two volumes under the title: *Law, The State, and The International Community* (1939-40), volume one of which constituted "A Commentary on the Development of Legal, Political, and International Ideals" and volume two a collection of quotations from the writings of those political and legal thinkers whose ideas were discussed in the first volume, all arranged in a subject order of his own making. Volume two he called in the looser meaning of the term a "codification" of political and legal conceptions influential in the modern world. His personal archive contains a large body of working papers and drafts drawn up over the years in connection with various activities, not least the preparation of *The Catholic Conception of International Law*. Whether he was able to take full advantage of this material when approaching the Vatican about incorporating international law into the syllabi of Catholic secondary and higher education or not, he made good and extensive use of these materials in this, his last, major work.

A chapter is devoted in the Commentary to Vitoria ("the founder, in the opinion of many, of the modern law of nations") and Suarez ("the prince of modern jurists"), but the influence of the progenitors of the "Spanish School" in this study is much larger when the chapter is read against the accompanying volume of documents. When Scott sent the volume to press, the Suarez works had not yet appeared in the "Classics of International Law" series and indeed were published in 1944 shortly after James Brown Scott died. But he had the manuscript of Suarez by then and was disposed to use that resource extensively: "It may ... seem, especially to those who are not familiar with Francisco Suarez, that the number of quotations from his writings is disproportionately large. And it is quite true that more passages have been drawn from Suarez than from any other writer" (p. ix). The reason for this, Scott says, is not his partiality on his part towards the Catholic jurists, but to the fact that "... in certain of his writings, especially in his great

Tractatus de legibus ac Deo legislatore, there is summed up and blended into a philosophic whole the best of our legal and our political heritage from the ancient and medieval worlds".

The Declaration of the Rights and Duties of Nations adopted by the American Institute of State and Law at its inaugural meeting epitomizes the principles and conceptions motivating so much of James Brown Scott's activities as a scholar and practitioner of international law. He believed deeply in the American experience being relevant to all nations of the world as embodied in the Constitution of the United States and in the judicial practice of the United States Supreme Court. More eloquent an apostle of those views is difficult to identify among American international lawyers. His turn towards Latin America may or may not have been an extension of his interest in the contributions of the "Spanish School" to the origins of modern international legal doctrine, but his deep affection for that profoundly neglected portion of the western hemisphere is transparent in all of his activities connected with the American Institute of International Law. With his departure from the scene, Latin America lost a friend who has proved to be irreplaceable.

The
American Institute of International Law:

Its Declaration of the Rights and Duties of Nations

By

JAMES BROWN SCOTT
President of the American Institute of International Law

Le premier et le plus grand intérêt est toujours la justice. Tous veulent que les conditions soient égales pour tous, et la justice n'est que cette égalité. Le citoyen ne veut que les lois et que l'observation des lois. Chaque particulier dans le peuple sait bien que, s'il y a des exceptions, elles ne seront pas en sa faveur. Ainsi tous craignent les exceptions; et qui craint les exceptions aime la loi.

JEAN JACQUES ROUSSEAU.

THE AMERICAN INSTITUTE OF INTERNATIONAL LAW
WASHINGTON, D. C.
1916

FOREWORD

The American Institute of International Law, which met at Washington in connection with and under the auspices of the Second Pan American Scientific Congress, adopted on January 6, 1916, a Declaration of the Rights and Duties of Nations. The Declaration differs from other projects of a like kind in that it is not based solely, or indeed at all, upon philosophic principles, but is based exclusively upon decisions of the Supreme Court of the United States. It is therefore fair to say that the principles of the Declaration are, as far as the United States is concerned, the law of the land, and an examination of the practice of the other American countries shows that these principles obtain in each of the American Republics, so that the Declaration is in reality a statement of the fundamental principles of international law, as they are understood in the New World.

At the tenth annual meeting of the American Society of International Law, held in Washington, D. C., on April 26, 1916, the Honorable Elihu Root, President of the Society, devoted his opening address to a consideration of the Declaration, its principles, and their importance.*

During the session of the American Institute, the undersigned, who happens to be its President, delivered a series of addresses dealing largely with the ideas contained in the preamble of the Declaration, without which it is incomplete. It has been thought advisable to print the series of addresses, just referred to, in connected form, as an introduction to the Declaration, and to follow it with the official commentary, which the Institute adopted at one and the same time with the text of the Declaration.

For the convenience of those who may be interested in the American Institute of International Law, its constitution and by-laws, its list of members and officers are placed in an appendix.

JAMES BROWN SCOTT.

Washington, D. C., June 3, 1916.

---

*Mr. Root's address is printed in the Proceedings of the American Society of International Law (1916), pp. 1–11; American Journal of International Law, vol. 10, pp. 211–221; Root's Addresses on International Subjects (1916), pp. 413–426.

TABLE OF CONTENTS

APPENDIX

The
American Institute of International Law

Its Declaration of the Rights and
Duties of Nations

Mr. Secretary of State, Mr. Ambassador, Mr. Root, Members
of the American Institute of International Law:

His Excellency the Secretary of State of the United States,
whom we are happy to count as a member, has welcomed the
Institute on behalf of the Government of the United States.
His Excellency the Chilean Ambassador, likewise a member, has welcomed it on behalf of the Second Pan American Scientific Congress, of which he is the worthy President; and Mr. Elihu Root, Honorary President of the Institute, and friend of all the Americas, has welcomed it on
behalf of the publicists of North America, of whom he
is the most distinguished representative. It becomes my
very great pleasure, on behalf of the Institute, whose President I am for the time being, to thank you for the generous
welcome which you have extended, to express our grati-
tude for the confidence which you have shown by your presence
in our ability to carry out the purposes for which the Institute was created, and to voice our appreciation of your
commendation, which encourages us to hope, if not to believe,
that we may, in some slight measure, be worthy of the rôle
which your generosity ascribes to us in the development of
international law in the American continent.

It is also my very great pleasure, on behalf of the Institute,
to welcome the charter members and the representatives of
the twenty-one national societies who have been delegated to
attend its opening session, and to express its grateful recognition of the interest which the national societies have shown by
delegating such distinguished publicists to take part in its
proceedings; and, on behalf of the Institute, I congratulate you upon the enthusiasm which has led you to come such
great distances to take part in the proceedings of a scientific
body, which has yet, if I may use a knightly expression, to win
its spurs. It is especially gratifying to us that you have re-
sponded so generously and so promptly, and, in behalf of the

founders and of the officers of the Institute, I congratulate you
and I thank you.

Why should the Secretary of State of the United States, the
Chilean Ambassador and President of the Congress, and
the most distinguished of North American statesmen welcome
the Institute and take part in its formal opening, and why
should representatives of the national societies of international
law of every American country come to Washington from the
most distant portions of the continent in order to spend a day,
as it were, in conference with publicists of the twenty-one
American republics? What is the nature of this Institute which
has been formally opened in their presence? What are its
aims and purposes, that busy men should concern themselves
with it? What is the field of its activities and what services
can it be expected to render which would justify the presence
of so many and of such eminent publicists?

The Formation and Object of the American Institute of International Law

In simplest terms, the American Institute of International
Law was intended to, and will, it is to be hoped, give visible
form and shape to the one great interest which the American
republics have in common, namely, the interest that the
principles of justice, common alike to all and which determine the rights and duties of the men and women of each of
the American republics, may become the standard of right and
of wrong between and among the American republics, and that
while measuring their rights they shall likewise prescribe their
duties one with another. The American Institute of International Law is a frank and unqualified recognition of the fact
that there is neither great nor small, rich nor poor, in the eyes
of justice; that all are equal, that all have equal duties, that all
have equal rights, and that the duties and the rights are the
same for all; that what is right for one can not be wrong for
another, and that what is inherently wrong can not possibly be
right, even although the republic involved be the most numer-

ously peopled and the greatest in physical power. It proclaims the equality in law and before law of all the American republics. It insists that each has a like interest in the triumph of right and in the repression of wrong. It asserts in the language of Chief Justice Marshall, that "no nation can make a rule for others" and that "none can make a law of nations," from which it necessarily follows that the law to regulate the conduct of the Americas must be made by the Americas; that the law of nations must be made, not by any one nation, but by all nations. It is in the belief that the intellectual is preëminently the one field in which the American peoples can coöperate without fear and without hesitation; it is with the example of the services which the Institute of International Law has rendered to the cause of international justice, and it is also with the hope that American publicists can render a not unlike service to the American republics, if not to the society of nations as a whole, that the American Institute of International Law was formed and composed of representatives of the national societies of international law created in each of the twenty-one American republics.

It has been formally opened in the presence of representatives of every society of international law of every American republic, in the presence of the Secretary of State of the United States, of the President of the Congress, and of the distinguished North American statesman, because American publicists feel the need of a central and a directing force to be their agent and subject to their control, and because they further feel that the Institute, which is their agent, can perform these services; that the Institute and the societies of international law affiliated with it and working together and in harmony can both develop and popularize that system of international law without which, and without whose observance, anarchy rears its ugly head and tramples under foot the civilization, which alone is thinkable, and which can thrive only in an atmosphere of confidence and under the protection of just laws.

The American Institute of International Law begins its

career today and it is for its members to say whether it will justify its creation, or rather, it is for its members to make it worthy of its self-imposed mission, to develop and to make known the principles of international law, based upon justice, which must control the actions of the American republics in their relations one with another, if justice is to prevail in the western world.

The plan to form the Institute was the plan of two citizens of the two republics farthest apart, for one came from the most southern republic of South America and the other from the most northern republic of North America. The two enthusiasts, for they must needs have been enthusiasts to believe that, though dwelling so far apart they might nevertheless come together in the realm of ideals, met in the city of Washington in the month of May, 1911, to discuss questions of a like interest to the American republics, just as we meet today, again in the city of Washington, to discuss these same questions, and to devise means for realizing the ideals in practice which are before our eyes and in our hearts. They came to the conclusion that, in order to have justice leaven the American continent, a society of international law should be formed by the publicists of each republic, that there should be formed an American Institute of International Law in which each national society should be represented by an equal number of members, and that the Institute, coöperating with each of the societies, should give direction to their efforts and acceptable form to their deliberations.

They were, however, unwilling to surrender their judgment to what might be called their enthusiasm, and they addressed themselves to Mr. Root—happily with us today, and testifying his confidence in the Institute for which he also is responsible—saying, in a letter written on the 3d day of June, 1911, "after reflection and very much discussion of the advantages and the difficulties of such an undertaking, we, however, reached the conclusion that the best way to draw the leaders of thought together would be to create an American Institute of International Law, in which the publicists of each country should be represented, say, by five members; that the publicists of each American country should organize in their capital a local society of international law; that the American Institute should hold periodical meetings, the first of which should be held in Washington, for the scientific discussion of questions of international law, especially those relating to peace, so that little by little a code of international law might be drafted which would represent the enlightened thought of the American publicists and be the result of their sympathetic coöperation." To this appeal, Mr. Root, as an American in whose conception of America there is neither North nor South, could not and did not turn a deaf ear. He approved the project and placed himself unreservedly at their disposition.

Although greatly encouraged by the outspoken approval of Mr. Root, the enthusiasts—because people are enthusiasts or are considered as such until they have realized their ideals— were nevertheless unwilling to ask the coöperation of their fellow-publicists of the American republics until they had satisfied themselves beyond peradventure that the project, if realized, would justify the efforts necessary to call it into being. They felt that European publicists could be counted upon to approach the question in a spirit of detachment, if not in a critical spirit, and that the judgment of the members of the Institute of International Law would be peculiarly valuable because of the experience which they had had in the study of international problems and in the development of international law. The European publicists without exception approved the formation of the Institute, in the belief that, if formed, it might render genuine services to the cause of international law in the western world, and they thereby greatly strengthened the confidence of the two enthusiasts in the feasibility of their project and the advisability of its realization.

The proposers of the new Institute were thus assured of a widespread belief in its usefulness if it could be founded.

It was evident that its formation would depend upon the coöperation of the publicists of the different American states, and that it could only be created if leaders of thought in the different countries would confer one with another and agree to take the steps necessary to call into being the national societies upon which the Institute must rest. The proposers therefore addressed themselves to those publicists in the different American countries whom they happened to know and who, they believed—and the event justified their belief,—would enter into the project as if it were their own and procure its realization. They prepared a confidential note, which they sent to one publicist in each of the American states, explaining in brief terms the nature and purpose of the Institute and asking for an expression of opinion.

It would be unfair to say that the publicists consulted were in favor of the project; they were enthusiastic over it; and, encouraged by the approval of Mr. Root, of the European publicists and of representative publicists from each of the American republics, the founders of the Institute felt justified in taking the steps which were in their opinion necessary to secure its establishment. These steps were the creation in each of the American republics of a national society of international law, which, when created, should express a desire to be affiliated with the proposed American Institute of International Law, to be composed of five publicists from each of the national societies, elected by the charter members of the Institute upon the recommendation of the national societies. In this way, we were not imposing something from above, and we were not asking the publicists to coöperate with us in the formation of a body which should more or less resemble the other Institute. We were asking the publicists of the twenty-one American republics to consider themselves as one great family, to divide themselves for purposes of convenience into twenty-one different groups, and to have the Institute as the committee, so to speak, of the American publicists thus divided into twenty-one groups or twenty-one national societies.

It was evident that the publicists as a whole could not come together at any one time and at any one place without great difficulty and without great inconvenience; it was equally evident that the publicists of any one country would feel more disposed to devote themselves to the study of international law and to the dissemination of its rules if they were gathered together into a society of their own making and within their own country. But the proposers of the Institute recognized that the grouping of the publicists would fail of its purpose unless each group were considered as a part of a larger whole, for, although a society is national in respect to location and composed of members of one and the same country, it should nevertheless be and feel itself to be part of a larger body; and all questions of interest to and affecting the foreign relations of any one nation must be considered from the standpoint of all other nations, inasmuch as a right claimed by one can not be denied by another nation and a right admitted to belong to one is a duty of all to observe and indeed of all to protect. In international relations a right can not stand alone. It is accompanied by a duty so closely allied that right and duty are not considered as separate and distinct, but as two faces of one and the same thing, like the two faces of the coin which passes current.

The best if not the only way to create this international feeling, which an American educator has happily called the "international mind," is to suggest not merely that each society is a part of a larger whole, but that each society is incomplete in itself and that without association with the others it fails of its purpose. How is this sentiment to be created? Shall it radiate, as it were, from a common center, like the spokes of a wheel; or, on the contrary, shall these different national societies create a central organization which shall not be above them, because it is in a way their creation or depends upon their existence, and is to be regarded as their agent and the agency of the American publicists in giving a central direction, in coördinating the efforts of the societies and generalizing, while harmonizing, their views? In other words, if the society is to be the national element, should not this central agency be the international element, at the same time in which it is the point of union and the clearing house, as it were, of the views of the national societies? How was this to be done? While recognizing the independence of each society, the principle of solidarity, which is an American doctrine, suggested, if it did not require, a federation of these national societies. A federation in the western world is only thinkable in terms of equality. To an American this seemed to be as natural as it was easy, and no institute of international law could be founded in this continent with hopes of success upon any other principle. Therefore, the founders of the Institute proposed that a national society should be formed in each of the American republics; that, although separate and distinct, each should recognize its dependence upon the other; that a central body or organization should be formed by the choice of an equal number of publicists from each of the American societies elected by the Institute, upon the recommendation of each of the national societies.

It is unnecessary to trace step by step the measures taken to create these national centers, and to unite them, though not to merge them, through their representatives, in a central organization. Suffice it to say that through the coöperation of the charter members in each of the American countries; through Mr. Root's approval of the plan and the confidence of the American publicists in the rectitude, disinterestedness and soundness of his judgment; through Mr. Bacon's visit to various South American countries, in which he advocated the formation of national societies of international law, to be affiliated with the Institute; through Mr. Lansing's intervention in his private capacity with his colleagues, the ministers of foreign affairs of the different American states, and through the coöperation of the governments of these states, in many instances, a national society was formed in every American republic, to be affiliated with the American Institute. Publicists

were chosen to represent the national societies in this opening
session of the Institute, and members were recommended for
election as representatives of the national societies in the Institute. Because of the interest evidenced by your presence, the
American Institute of International Law has ceased to be a
project, in becoming a fact.

Without further dwelling upon these matters, which are
known to us all, let me quote one article of the Constitution,
which, having met with the approval of the national societies,
is the official statement of our aims and purposes. Article II
of the Constitution is thus worded:

The American Institute of International Law is an
unofficial scientific association.

It proposes:

1. To give precision to the general principles of international law as they now exist, or to formulate new ones,
in conformity with the solidarity which unites the members of the society of civilized nations, in order to
strengthen these bonds and, especially, the bonds between
the American peoples;

2. To study questions of international law, particularly
questions of an American character, and to endeavor to
solve them, either in conformity with generally accepted
principles, or by extending and developing them, or by
creating new principles adapted to the special needs of the
American Continent;

3. To discover a method of codifying the general or
special principles of international law, and to elaborate
projects of codification on matters which lend themselves thereto;

4. To aid in bringing about the triumph of the principles of justice and of humanity which should govern the
relations between peoples, considered as nations, through
more extensive instruction in international law, particularly in American universities, through lectures and
addresses, as well as through publications and all other
means;

5. To organize the study of international law along
truly scientific and practical lines in a way that meets the

needs of modern life, and taking into account the problems of our hemisphere and American doctrines;

6. To contribute, within the limits of its competence and the means at its disposal, toward the maintenance of peace, or toward the observance of the laws of war and the mitigation of the evils thereof;

7. To increase the sentiment of fraternity among the Republics of the American Continent, so as to strengthen friendship and mutual confidence among the citizens of the countries of the New World.

International Law is a Branch of Jurisprudence and Should Be Studied and Developed as Such

It will be noted that the fifth object of the Institute, as stated in the Constitution, is "to organize the study of international law along truly scientific and practical lines in a way that meets the needs of modern life, and taking into account the problems of our hemisphere and American doctrines." I may be pardoned, in view of the importance of the subject, if I seem to digress in order to offer some observations upon the study of international law.

To study international law, we must needs form a clear conception of international law; otherwise its study would be of little, if any, value, and in any event it would be impossible to study it scientifically as the Institute requires. Now, if I am correct in the contention that international law is international right, that is to say, that it is justice, applied to and by nations, and if I am further correct in the contention that the fundamental principles of justice are common alike to national as well as to international law, we have a standard by which to measure international justice and we likewise have a method by which its principles may be imparted; because we are familiar with the fundamental principles of national justice and we have had a long experience in the scientific study and in imparting a knowledge of these principles.

We are justified in asserting that international law is law. If it were necessary to quote authority for this assertion we could point to the decision of the Supreme Court of the United

States in the case of the *Paquete Habana*, decided in January, 1900, in which Mr. Justice Gray, speaking for the court, said:

> International law is part of our law, and must be ascertained and administered by the courts of justice of appropriate jurisdiction, as often as questions of right depending upon it are duly presented for their determination.

In order that the nature of international law and its status in the United States should be made clear, the learned justice enumerated as follows the sources of international law:

> For this purpose, where there is no treaty, and no controlling executive or legislative act or judicial decision, resort must be had to the customs and usages of civilized nations; and, as evidence of these, to the works of jurists and commentators, who by years of labor, research and experience, have made themselves peculiarly well acquainted with the subjects of which they treat. Such works are resorted to by judicial tribunals, not for the speculations of their authors concerning what the law ought to be, but for trustworthy evidence of what the law really is.[1]

Armed with this decision, we do not need to debate whether international law is or should be law, or to discuss its sources; because, however fallible a court may be, it is to be presumed that the Supreme Court of the United States, composed as it is of nine thoughtful and experienced lawyers, sworn to administer the law of the land, are more likely to be right than a mere theorist who speaks on his own authority and on his own responsibility, or than a foreign office whose views are colored and indeed moulded by policy.

If, then, international law is law, or is to be considered as law, it follows that it is a branch of jurisprudence and that it should be taught as is law and as is jurisprudence. Now, an analysis of national law shows that it is made up of rules

---

[1] 175 United States Reports, 677, 700.

devised with more or less success to give effect to principles of justice; that these rules are statements of rights and of duties, although the statement of a right carries with it the duty of others to recognize and to observe the right, for the right of one is the duty of all to observe, and a duty of one involves a right also to the performance of this duty, for duty and right are correlative. But a statement of rights and of duties is one thing; their observance is quite another thing. They are not self-executing. There must be some means of enforcing a right, and of redressing a wrong which is a violation of this right.

If we take a specific example, the idea which I have in mind may become clearer. Let us consider, for example, the law of contracts, or, what is very frequently called in systems based upon Roman law, the law of obligations. Now, the law of contracts is made up of the statement of rights and duties, and the law thereof is so taught. What is a contract? Who may contract? What is an offer? What an acceptance? When is a particular offer accepted? When is there such a meeting of the minds as to result in a contract or an obligation? In the language of analytical jurisprudence, these and many other principles form substantive law. But it is a very practical world in which we live. It generally has a reason for what it does and it is averse to the study of things which have no apparent utility. The right is therefore considered useless if it can not be exercised; the duty meaningless if it can not be compelled. Therefore, alongside of rights there are remedies, or the rules of procedure to enforce rights and duties and to obtain redress for wrongs. In the language of analytical jurisprudence, these rules taken together form what is known as adjective law. But substantive law is one thing, and procedure quite another thing; and confusion results or is likely to result unless they be kept separate and distinct.

If international law is law and if it is made up of rules creating rights and imposing duties, it would seem that these rights and duties should be stated as they are in systems of law, and that the procedure by which rights are maintained, duties enforced, and wrongs redressed should be considered separate and distinct from substantive rights, because they are separate and distinct. If international law is considered as law, and as a branch of jurisprudence, it should be taught as such; its substantive rules should be disengaged from the rules of procedure and expounded as in the case of a branch of national law; and the rules of procedure should likewise be separated as they are in national law and expounded as a system of procedure applicable to the law of nations. The result would be a classification of the substantive principles of international law, similar to although not necessarily identical with the classification of private law, because we are dealing with states, that is, artificial persons, and not with the natural persons of private law. When we come to the matter of procedure, we see that this part of the law is very defective and that agencies and remedies which are regarded, and rightly so, as essential in national law are either wholly lacking in international law, or are rudimentary in the sense that they are only coming into being. Such a classification would make the time-honored division of international law into the law of peace and war meaningless, because there is no law of peace and there is no law of war as such. They are rules which, taken together, define and state the rights and duties of nations. There are two methods of enforcing these rights and duties and of redressing wrongs. One is peaceful in the sense that it does not involve a resort to force disturbing the order of the community. The other differs in that it involves a resort to force which disturbs the ordinary life of the communities immediately affected, and, in a lesser degree, the world at large. This, although called war, is in essence self-redress by self-directed force. Now, in every nation making a pretense to civilization, self-redress has been tried and found wanting. Courts of justice have been created in which differences of a justiciable nature between man and man are decided, not by the litigants themselves, not by a resort to force, but by disinterested persons called judges, who ascertain the principles of justice applicable to the case and decide by the impartial application of such principles.   Self-redress, which has been banished from within civilized society, flourishes between states.   It is a survival of what is justly considered barbarism within states, and it can not be other than barbarism between states.   This method of separating international law into substantive law, on the one hand, and remedial law, on the other, has the great advantage of treating the remedies separate and distinct from the rights, and of showing that war, at best a remedy, must give way to that better remedy which, except as between states, has everywhere supplanted self-redress.

We know that the rule of national law does not always lie upon the surface or at hand; that in many cases we must seek for it as for hidden treasure, and that it is only found after much search and difficulty.   We also know that when a principle of law is found it must be interpreted and applied to the concrete case, and we know that, in interpreting it and applying it to the concrete case, law is insensibly, but none the less certainly developed.   We have had centuries of experience in the teaching of law, in the finding of law, in the interpretation of law, and in the development of law; and the knowledge, the skill, and the methods devised through these centuries of experience can be turned to the profit of nations if international law is law; because if it is or is considered as such, it naturally follows that the experience had in other branches of law can be availed of in the matter of ascertaining, interpreting, and developing international law.

Again, we know that the greatest possible agency in the development of a system of law is the court.   We know that law is not studied in law schools merely for mental discipline; that the business of the world is regulated by law; that the rights and duties of men in their business relations are defined by law, and that honest differences of opinion, not to speak of disputes of a questionable origin and nature are carried into court where the facts involved are found, where lawyers, intent upon the success of their client's cause, press a rule of law upon judges who, indifferent to the dispute and sworn to administer justice impartially, adjudge the case according to law.

We say that courts administer law, but that they do not make it; that it is the duty of the legislature to make or modify the law. This is no doubt true, and yet it is questionable if a court really can exist and administer justice without making law. We therefore speak of the law made by courts as judge-made law, and there is a widespread opinion that the law made by judges is better and more satisfactory than the law made by legislatures. In any event, in the English-speaking world, this is so, and the rules of the common law of England have, in the course of centuries, been moulded, developed and given the symmetry of a code by English judges. Is it too much to hope, to expect, indeed to believe, that the common law of nations can be moulded, developed and given the precision of a code by international judges sitting in international courts of justice?

International Law is or Should Be Made Synonymous with International Right

Before leaving this phase of the subject, I desire to call your attention to a matter which may be thought to be academic, but which I venture to think is well-nigh fundamental.

It will be observed that, in the leading European languages, the term meaning *right* is used to designate international law, whereas in English we use, in connection with international law, a term which may or may not be synonymous with *right*, but which is not necessarily synonymous with it. Thus, in French we speak indifferently of *droit des gens* or *droit international;* in Spanish, of *derecho de gentes* or *derecho internacional;* in Italian, of *diritto di gentes* or *diritto internazionale;* in German, of *Völkerrecht* or *Internationales Recht.* Likewise in English we speak indifferently of the *law of nations* or of *international law,* but in so doing the word *law* is used in each case.

Now, the word *law* is ambiguous, and it is doubtful in English whether law means right or justice, or merely something imposed or commanded, whether right or wrong. This is not only a matter of form; it is one of substance. It is the distinction between *jus* and *lex,* expressing different conceptions by different words between that which is intrinsically right and that which is enacted by statute. The European phraseology means and can only mean that *right* is the basis, and that international law is but the formulation of the rules which express and which are designed to apply the conception of international right. If we bear this in mind, international *law* is international *right.* It is the right based upon justice, which varies but little with time and place, to which the measured and weighty phrase of Cicero is applicable:

> Neque erit alia lex Romae, alia Athenis, alia nunc, alia posthac; sed et *omnes gentes* et omni tempore *una lex* et sempiterna et immutabilis contenebit, unusque erit communis quasi magister et imperator omnium Deus.

If these views be correct, justice is much the same thing the world over. An examination of the principles of the law of each state shows that they are substantially the same, and this fact should lead us to believe that the principles of justice, common to all peoples within their national boundaries, may be accepted as the principles of justice to be applied between the states, made up of peoples sharing these fundamental conceptions. Our duty then is to adopt as a basis these principles of justice, which, taken together, make up international right, and to formulate the rules of conduct between and among nations which express and which are designed to apply the conception of international right. These rules may differ according to the skill with which the principles of justice are discovered and incorporated in them; but a common standard of international right is bound to produce a common rule which will be an outward and visible expression of a universal and therefore international right. The purpose of the American Institute in studying the law of nations should be and doubtless will be to discover and to disclose the justice common to all, and to formulate the rules of conduct between states which express and which are designed to apply the conception of international justice.

Law in Peace Not Law of War Is the Chief Concern of the American Institute of International Law

Having explained the purposes which the founders of the American Institute had in proposing its establishment, having detailed the steps which were taken to call it into being in the different American republics, and, having stated the favorable opinions of the European publicists who were consulted and their views as to the services which the Institute could render, it would seem that the policy which we should pursue is clearly indicated, and that we only need to rear our structure upon the foundations already laid, in the consciousness that these very foundations must in large part determine the nature of the edifice which we hope will assume definite form and shape in your hands. We must bear in mind that our members, although not recruited from any one country, as is the case with national societies, are nevertheless recruited from one continent. The projects which we may devise will therefore be international, because they will be discussed and will be adopted by the representatives of twenty-one nations; but these twenty-one nations, although sovereign, independent and equal, are not scattered over the world. They are the twenty-one republics which, taken together, form the western hemisphere, and, in view of their origin and of the principles which they profess, they are aptly termed the New World.

Separated as we are from other continents by the Atlantic and Pacific Oceans, which in the past at least have been barriers, although in the future they may be found to connect the new world with the far east and the far west, it may well be that the principles which we seek to establish will be continental without ceasing to be international; and that the projects which we adopt will make a special appeal to the nations of the western continent, because, try as we will, we can not wholly detach ourselves from our national interests and from our national conditions.   As each republic is represented in the Institute by an equal number of publicists, recommended by the national society of each republic and representing that society, it follows that the views of the publicists of each country will be made known to the Institute, that they will be considered by its members in reaching conclusions, and that no project will be, can be, or should be adopted which is inconsistent with the conditions and traditions, the hopes or aspirations of the continent which is in years, but still more in its principles, in its point of view and in its ideals, a new world.

Now, without meaning to suggest that wars have not taken place and that they will not again break out in the western hemisphere, it is a fact that the republics of this continent are addicted to peace rather than to war, that peace is the rule, war the exception, and that when the resort is made to arms it generally happens that the war is civil, rather than international.   The causes of the resort to arms, therefore, can ordinarily be ascribed to an imperfect internal organization in which the checks and balances so necessary in constitutional law and in national life have not been devised, or do not produce that order and equilibrium which in international life or which between states we would call peace.   The problem with which we as American publicists are confronted is primarily to find or to hit upon a standard of conduct and a measure or test thereof which, recognizing the sovereignty, the independence, and the equality of every American state, will subject each and every one of them to this standard of conduct and by it test their actions.

It will not escape notice that the founders of the Institute have, in their various communications on the subject and in their draft of a constitution, stated in no uncertain terms that peace is to have the lion's share of attention, and that the rules and regulations concerning warfare are not to be the chief object of their solicitude. They believe that peace is the outcome of justice and that in their opinion a *pax americana* can only flow from justice and its application between and among American peoples. Therefore, our preoccupation is to study the fundamental principles of justice; to endeavor to show that they are applicable between nations as well as between individuals; that they are translatable into terms of international law and that these principles of justice, not the rules and regulations of war, form the branch of jurisprudence which we call the law of nations. That these principles of justice, which in their application produce peace and which form what may be called the substantive law of nations, have been neglected by publicists for the study of the rules and regulations of war, which are at most a remedy to enforce rights and to redress wrongs, is evident to the casual observer, and has never been better put than it was some sixty years ago by the distinguished German publicist and statesman Robert von Mohl, who said:

> Just as international law has already developed the laws of war and of bloody compulsion to an infinitely greater extent than the laws of peaceful intercourse, even so has the science of politics directed its efforts to that part of international relations characterized by brute force and cunning. This is undeniably a heavy debt which science must make good.[1]

Justice Is the Bond of Men in and Between States

It is poor policy to lock the stable door after the horse has been stolen. It is indeed necessary to send for the doctor when the patient is sick, but today we lay great stress, and rightly, upon preventive medicine. We think of war as a disease in it-

---

[1] Encyklopädie der Staatswissenschaften (1859), p. 704.

self. It is not. It is the external symptom of an internal disorder of the body politic, and the proper thing to do is not merely to denounce war, to take measures to prevent its outbreak, and to regulate its conduct, but to probe beneath the surface to discover and to remove the evils which, if undiscovered or unremoved, will inevitably result in war. Now, no nation can be above the experience of mankind, and the experience of mankind in every country belonging to the society of nations is that justice between man and man is the essential condition of order, that the presence of justice prevents disorder, and that its administration maintains peace in the community. These ideas are commonplaces, for which no authority is needed. If, however, authority be desired, it is as ancient as Aristotle, who says in that oldest and yet newest of treatises on Politics, that "justice is the bond of men in states, and the administration of justice, which is the determination of what is just, is the principle of order in political society." If justice is the bond of men in states, and we know from daily experience that it is, we may one day find by experience that justice is not merely the bond of men in states but the bond between states, or, to speak in terms of international law, that justice is the bond between nations. For, after all, states are made up of men and women held together by the bond of justice. As Sir William Jones, distinguished as scholar, jurist and poet, puts it:

What constitutes a state?
.   .   .   .
Men who their duties know,
But know their rights, and knowing, dare maintain.
.   .   .   .
And sovereign law, that state's collected will,
O'er thrones and globes elate,
Sits empress, crowning good, repressing ill.

This justice, however, must be administered and before this can be done it must needs be determined, for, as Aristotle says, although his authority is not needed and I quote him merely to show that the ideas which I venture to express are as old as the hills, "justice is the principle of order in political society."

Now, let us reason together and let us see where an analysis of this simple sentence—for it is only a sentence—will bring us. An association of men and women within certain territorial limits, be they large or small, with articles of association regulating the conduct of each toward the other within territorial boundaries, creates a community, which is only another way of saying that the men and women thus associated and thus considered form a unit and that the community or unit is a political one. The principle of order in this political society is justice. If order be the result of justice, then the continuance of that order depends upon the continuous administration of justice. If justice be the bond of men in states, the continuous administration of justice is the continuous bond; if justice be the bond of men in states, it follows that justice is the bond of men in each and every state, because no distinction is made between state and state; if justice be the bond between men within each of these states, it follows, if the principles of justice be similar or identical, that justice will be common to the men and women of each state, consequently to the men and women of all states; if it be the principle of order in one state, it will be the principle of order in all states holding this common conception of justice, and its administration will maintain the principle of order which justice and its administration created.

If these statements be accepted, and they can not well be rejected, we find it necessary to agree upon certain things, in order that justice may be the bond and its administration maintain order between and among the states of the American continent. We must be clear in our minds as to what we mean by states. We must be clear in our minds as to what we mean by justice. We must be clear in our minds as to what we mean by its administration, and we must provide some machinery for its ascertainment and for its administration between states, if justice is to be the bond in international society as it is in national societies. We must not deceive ourselves as to the far-reaching effect of these simple statements, which may perhaps be admitted in the abstract, but to whose consequences, applied in the concrete, many may object. A little thought and reflection will make this very clear and show how step by step we are led to the conclusion that states, like the men and women composing them, are subjected to the rules of law and the principles of justice common alike to men and states. If the principles of Aristotle be admitted, this conclusion seems inevitable, because, if justice is the bond of men in states, and if justice and its administration are the principle of order in political society, it follows as the night the day that, not only should the relations of men to men be determined by principles of justice, but that the relations of men to men, on the one hand, and to the state which they have formed on the other should also be regulated by the principles of justice. From this point of view, men formed political societies, and, practicing the precept of Aristotle, the statesmen of the American Revolution ordained justice, as set forth in the preamble to the Constitution of the United States, and also provided apt agencies for its administration.

The Conception of the American State Is Based upon the Declaration of Independence of the United States

We of America do not need to trouble ourselves about the original state, if there were an original state, or, indeed, how the different states of Europe came into existence. We take our stand upon a continent and that continent a new world, not indeed from the physical standpoint, which we could not maintain, but from the intellectual and political standpoint. We know how each of the American states came into being. We know that high-minded men assembled in each of the twenty-one republics of our western continent, represented officially today in the Pan American Scientific Congress and unofficially, but none the less really, in the American Institute, in order to create a political society for themselves, separate and distinct from that of the European countries whereof they were the colonists, in the belief that they had the right, and by the exercise of it making it such, to form a state in each case; to determine the rules of law to regulate the rights and duties of the citizens or the inhabitants of each of the states thus formed, and to regulate the rights and duties of the government which in each case they created to promote order, happiness and well-being. When, again as the result of experience, the states which had thus been formed seemed to some of the people thereof to be too large, the larger were broken into smaller states.

It is not necessary for me to go into details or to recount the process by which this happened, as it is familiar in its great lines to all of us. Let me content myself, therefore, with a single instance, that of the United States, which happens to be the oldest and which has in some sense served as a model to all. For reasons which it is unnecessary to mention in this connection, the English colonists in North America decided to set up for themselves as the United States of America. They apparently had no doubt as to their right to do so; they had no doubt as to the position which their state was to assume among the then existing nations of the world; they had no doubt as to the nature of the state or of the political society, to use Aristotle's term, which they were creating; and as they stated their reasons in a document that he who runs may read, we are neither in doubt nor in the dark as to their aims and purposes. In the Declaration of Independence, proclaimed in Philadelphia on July 4, 1776, and which is stated to be the unanimous declaration of the thirteen United States of America, the members of the Congress apparently regarded it as the natural course of things for one section or group of people to separate itself from another. There was nothing mystic or hidden, divine or supernatural about it, because the separation which the founders of the Republic had in mind was to happen in the course of human, not of divine events. They felt that the separation, while it might be delayed, was destined to take place because they contemplate it as "necessary for one people to dissolve the political bands which have connected them with another," and the consequences of this separation enabled them "to assume among the Powers of the earth, the separate and equal station to which the Laws of Nature and of Nature's God entitle them." Now, although this separation was to happen in the course of human events, and to result in a political society separate and distinct from that of the mother-country, the framers of this declaration, feeling that the event was important and that the bonds connecting them should not be lightly severed, recounted the reasons in justification of what might appear extraordinary to the mother-country and dangerous in practice to other countries, because, as they said, "a decent respect to the opinions of mankind requires that they should declare the causes which impel them to the separation."

Every republic of the western continent has followed this example, and it would appear to be beyond the possibility of successful contradiction, that in this western world of ours the right of revolution or emancipation, to use the phraseology more common in the Latin American countries, exists. If it does not exist, we have no right to be here, and, if this theory of the origin of the state is not in accord with old world theories or books of authority, we should change the theory or discard the authority, rather than renounce our statehood. But the Declaration of Independence does not stop here, nor does it content itself with the mere statement of the causes which impelled separation, although those causes are set forth at great length. It defines the origin and nature of the state which the Declaration proclaimed; the origin and nature of the government and of the rights of the people creating and forming the state, and of the relations of the government to the people thus creating and forming the state. It first lays down certain rights possessed by the people, which the framers did not claim to create, but which they regarded as inherent in the people, so inherent indeed as to be inalienable; and it is to be noted that they did not take to themselves any credit for their discovery, because the existence of the rights was self-evident. "We hold," they said, "these truths to be self-evident, that all men are created equal, that they are endowed by their Creator with certain unalienable Rights, that among these are Life, Liberty and the pursuit of Happiness." This is not and could not well be a complete enumeration of the rights which men possess as men, and which were likewise self-evident and unalienable. These were, in their opinion, either the most important or the most important for their present purposes among others which they did not stop to mention. However numerous these fundamental rights might be, there was no doubt that they existed, that they could not be taken away, and that to maintain these rights and to protect the people in the enjoyment thereof, meaning thereby all rights as well as those specified, governments were created. It is to be observed that the expression "governments" is used in the Declaration in the plural as synonymous with states, and that "government" is used as synonymous with the machinery created within the state in order to maintain these rights in the particular state. The Declaration thus says: "that to secure these rights, Governments are instituted among Men, deriving their just powers from the consent of the governed." That is to say, men assembled for a political purpose and to create a political society which they call a state, to secure to them the enjoyment of the self-evident and unalienable rights. To maintain these rights within political society, men created some form of government, which, created by the people for a particular purpose, they unmake and make over according to their sovereign pleasure. Thus, "whenever any Form of Government becomes destructive of these ends, it is the Right of the People to alter or to abolish it, and to institute new Government, laying its foundation on such principles and organizing its powers in such form, as to them shall seem most likely to effect their Safety and Happiness."

I do not hold a brief for the theory of "natural rights." I neither claim that rights are inherent nor inalienable, but I do maintain that no conception of the state is or can be satis- factory to Americans which does not recognize the people of the American continent as possessed of these rights, and that no form of government will be tolerated by the American peoples which does not protect them in the enjoyment of these rights. The people of the United States find themselves in possession of these rights and they therefore regard them as "acquired" if they can not be said to be *natural or inherent* rights. And I further believe that the Government of the United States not only recognizes these rights, in so far as its citizens are concerned, but that it insists that governments in American countries in which the United States has influ- ence shall secure to the people thereof the protection and en- joyment of these rights. I do not, however, need to argue this point, because there is a precedent that speaks louder than words. Thus, Mr. Root, when Secretary of War and speaking for the United States, declared as a condition of the delivery of Cuba to its people "the maintenance of a govern- ment adequate to the protection of life, property and indi- vidual liberty," and he reserved, on behalf of the United States, the right to intervene in Cuba not only for the preser- vation of Cuban independence but for the maintenance of these specified rights.

It would seem to be beyond question that the framers of the Declaration of Independence recognized the right and the necessity of peoples to create states which, however, were not to be the masters but the servants of the creators, and that the forms of government instituted within the states were to be changed by the people thereof at any time and in any way which "as to them shall seem most likely to effect their Safety and Happiness." For, seeing that independence would result from the armed conflict between the Mother-Country and the colonists, our forefathers recognized that some step should be taken to form a government of the new states, and after the Declaration of Independence a form of government became necessary. In accordance therefore with the philosophy of that instrument, they created a confederation known as the United States of America, and the instrument of government drafted by the Congress in 1777 and approved by the last of the states in 1781 was known as the Articles of Confederation. This was the first conscious exercise of the right of the people of the American states to create a form of government, and, while it can not be said that it destroyed the rights which it was meant to serve, it is fair to say that it did not give satisfaction. Therefore, again appealing to the Declaration of Independence and the political philosophy which it contained, they exercised "the Right of the People to alter or to abolish" the form of government under the Articles of Confederation "and to institute new Government, laying its foundation on such principles and organizing its powers in such form, as to them shall seem most likely to effect their Safety and Happiness." Representatives of the states chosen for this purpose met in the city of Philadelphia in 1787 and devised a new form of government, laying its foundation on such principles and organizing its powers in such a way as to them seemed most likely to effect and which, for a century and more, has effected their safety and happiness.

Now, just as the framers of the Declaration of Independence felt that a decent respect to the opinions of mankind required a statement of the causes which impelled them to separation, the framers of the Constitution of the young states felt it necessary to proclaim to the people composing them the principles upon which the new government was framed, in accordance with the philosophy of the Declaration of Independence, and to assert in unmistakable terms that the Constitution was made by the people and for the people and subject to change by them, lest it might appear that the acceptance of the Constitution could possibly be construed as an abrogation of their rights. Thus, it is said in the preamble, that "the People of the United States, in Order to form a more-perfect Union"—for the union under the Confederation had been far from perfect—"establish justice, insure domestic Tranquility, provide for the common defence, promote the general welfare, and secure the Blessings of Liberty to our-selves and our Posterity, do ordain and establish this Consti-tution for the United States of America." The preamble is thus a conscious or an unconscious recognition of the princi-ple of Aristotle, confirmed by all human experience that "jus-tice is the bond of men in states"—the first purpose mentioned in the preamble is to establish justice—"and the administra-tion of justice, which is the determination of what is just, is the principle of order in political society."

The framers of the Constitution recognized the importance of their act; some of them had been signers of the Declara-tion of Independence and all of them knew what it meant. In the preamble to the work of their hands they stated their pur-pose in clear and unmistakable terms; for, as the great Chief Justice of the United States has said of them and of their handiwork, "as men whose intentions require no concealment generally employ the words which most directly and aptly ex-press the ideas they intend to convey, the enlightened patriots who framed our Constitution and the people who adopted it, must be understood to have employed words in their natural sense, and to have intended what they have said."[1] We know why they met in Philadelphia. We know what they tried to do and, better than they, we appreciate what they actually did. The journal of the convention has been published, the pro-ceedings in the conventions held in each of the states to con-sider and ratify the Constitution, are within the reach of all who may care to consult them, and at the distance of a cen-tury we can, as it were, open the door of the convention in Philadelphia where fifty-five honest, upright and experienced men labored at a constitution which was not merely to be the

---

[1]Gibbons vs. Ogden, 9 Wheaton, 1, 188.

instrument of government for them and their descendants, but a charter of government throughout the world.

> We know what Master laid thy keel,
> What Workmen wrought thy ribs of steel,
> Who made each mast, and sail, and rope,
> What anvils rang, what hammers beat,
> In what a forge and what a heat
> Were shaped the anchors of thy hope.

To the western world the state is the creature of known men, animated by a purpose likewise known and acting in accordance with the doctrines proclaimed in the Declaration of Independence of the United States, which is no longer the heritage of one people and of one country, but, unrestricted in place and in time, it is, as Thucydides would say, "a perpetual possession."

In the American Conception the State Is an Artificial Person, the Creature of the People and Subordinated to Law.

If the state is the creature of its people and if the state is created for certain purposes, it follows that the state can not be superior to the people creating it and that it can not properly be or become destructive of the ends for which it, as well as its form of government, was created. It is subordinated to its creators. Law prescribes the duties and safeguards the rights alike of men and of state, and of government as the agent of man within the state. There is a difference, it may be in form but not in substance. Man is a natural person, but subordinated to law in relation to his fellow men. The state, made up of men, subordinated to law in their mutual relations, is an artificial person, the creature of law and therefore subject to law, because, being artificial, it can not exist of itself, but must be created. It matters little, indeed it matters nothing, in law whether the natural person be large or small, rich or poor, wise or unwise. Under the law, each is the equal of all and under the Declaration of Independence all men are created equal. It matters little or nothing under law that the artificial person, whether it be a body politic which we call a state, or a corporation of an ordinary kind, be large or small, rich or poor, for each is the creature of law and is subordinated to the law of its creation.

Although I would rather not argue the question, I can not, in view of its importance, content myself with a mere statement. I feel that I must cite three authorities from among the many which might be selected, and I naturally choose the decisions of American courts of justice to lay down what must be considered an American, if we are not yet justified in holding it to be a universal, doctrine.

The first case is intended to show, and I believe it does show, that the colonists regarded the colony or province as a corporation, having a personality separate and distinct from that of the inhabitants composing it, and it explains how easily and naturally the same colonists considered the states which succeeded the colonies, and indeed the United States, as corporate bodies invested with the powers of a corporation and with a distinct, albeit artificial, personality.

The second case is intended to show, and I believe it does show, that, by association of states and without the action of a superior authority, a body politic comes into being, and as an artificial person this body politic is possessed of the rights of an artificial person.

The third case takes up the state where the second decision leaves it, and is intended to show, and I believe it does show, that the body politic, which we call the state in international law, is an artificial person and, as such, subject to the duties of an artificial person.

The first case to which I refer in this connection is entitled *Gray* v. *Paxton,* and was tried in the Province of Massachusetts Bay. On January 13, 1761, the House of Representatives "resolved that Harrison Gray, Esq., the Province Treasurer, be and hereby is empowered and directed to demand and receive the aforesaid sum of 475£, 9s, 11d of the respective persons from whom it shall appear to be due; and in case of their refusing or neglecting payment for the space of one month after demand, to bring an action or actions at common law for recovery of said sum, to the use of his Majesty, to be applied to the support of this Government as this court shall hereafter direct." The point which I wish to bring out by this case is admirably stated in a note of it made by John Adams, then at the Bar and later President of the United States, who says:

> Otis drew a writ *vs.* Paxton for Money had & received to the use of the Province. Prat pleaded in abatement, That, although the suit was brought in Gray's name, although Gray was Plaintiff, yet no promise was alleged to have been made to Gray. The Defendant is alleged to be indebted to the Province for money received to the Province's use, and to have promised to pay it to the Province, yet the Province is not Plaintiff. It is *Gray* v. *Paxton,* but it should have been *the Province of the Massachusetts Bay* v. *Paxton.*

The court decided in favor of the defendant for the reasons stated by Mr. Adams, namely, that Gray should have sued not in his own name but in the name and in behalf of the Province of the Massachusetts Bay, because, as Mr. Adams points out in a later passage, "a corporate body is one person in law and may sue or be sued."[1]

Now, the meaning of this is very simple. The Province of Massachusetts Bay was a corporation, endowed by law with personality, and the corporation, as Mr. Adams properly said, "may sue or be sued."

It is not necessary to rely upon unaided reasoning to sustain a contention that by the Declaration of Independence the states, called in that immortal document the United States of America, became in fact and in law a body politic possessing a distinct, although artificial, personality and enjoy-

---

[1] Quincy's Massachusetts Reports, 1761-1772, p. 546.

ing the rights appertaining to an artificial person. Nor is it necessary to refer to the Articles of Confederation forming a perpetual union of the states under the title of the United States of America, which became effective on and after March 1, 1781. Nor, finally, is it necessary to rely upon the holdings of the Supreme Court of the United States as to the nature of the union established by the Constitution of the United States, devised in Philadelphia in 1787, ratified by the people, and put into effect on the 4th day of March, 1789. We have a decision of the Supreme Court of Pennsylvania on the very point in question, decided in 1779, before the creation of a government for the erstwhile colonies under the Articles of Confederation or under the Constitution of the United States, which decision has never been questioned, much less overruled, recognizing that by the Declaration of Independence the United States became a body corporate or an artificial person. As this case is so interesting and so fundamental, and depends upon the reason of the thing (for the court had no precedent to guide it), I feel that I should state it somewhat at length.

The case in question is *Respublica* v. *Sweers*, decided in 1779, at the April term, by the Supreme Court of Pennsylvania, and found in the first volume of Dallas' Reports, at page 41. The defendant Sweers was a deputy Commissary General of Military Stores in the armies of the United States of America. As such, he was indicted in November, 1778, for forgery upon two bills "with intent to defraud the United States." The first indictment was for altering a receipt and the second was for forging a receipt. He was convicted upon both indictments, and his counsel took, as the report says, "several exceptions to the form and substance of these indictments, upon a motion in arrest of judgment." In pronouncing sentence, Mr. Chief Justice McKean, speaking for the Court, said:

> The first exception was, "that, at the time of the offense charged, the United States were not a body corpo-

rate known in law." But the court are of a different opinion. From the moment of their association, the United States necessarily became a body corporate; for, there was no superior from whom that character could otherwise be derived. In England, the king, lords and commons, are certainly a body corporate; and yet there never was any charter or statute, by which they were expressly so created.

Not only is the judgment interesting, but the form of the sentence attracts our attention, for, on the first indictment, the defendant was sentenced to "a fine of 70£ and imprisonment until the 4th of July, the anniversary of American Independence."

Respublica v. *Sweers* was a criminal case, and it is to be borne in mind that in cases of this kind the charge as made must be strictly proved, because every presumption is in favor of the innocency of the accused. The United States would not have been considered a political corporation by virtue of the Declaration of Independence, and before the Articles of Confederation had gone into effect, unless it had been clear beyond the possibility of successful contradiction that the United States, in fact and in law, was a corporation. It will be recalled that the first exception taken by defendant's counsel was "that at the time of the offense charged, the United States were not a body corporate known in law."

The third case to which I have referred, as showing that a state is an artificial person, or a corporation, and as such subordinated to the law affecting artificial persons or corporations, is doubly American, if this expression be permitted, because both the court trying the case and the state involved were American.

In the year 1889, the question arose in the Court of Appeals in the State of New York whether a state (in this case the Republic of Honduras) was to be considered as a foreign person or as a foreign corporation, which by the laws of New York was required to deposit security for costs before beginning a proceeding in a court of justice. In holding that a foreign nation was to be considered as a moral person or a foreign corporation and as such within the terms of the law, Chief Judge Ruger said:

> Section 3268 of the Code of Civil Procedure provides that a defendant, in an action brought in a court of record, may require security for costs, in cases, among others, where the plaintiff was, when the action was commenced, either "a person residing without the state"; or "a foreign corporation." The plaintiff claims to be a foreign independent state.
>
> It is urged by the plaintiff that it is neither a person nor a foreign corporation, within the meaning of the Code. It is not disputed but that the plaintiff is an independent government, recognized as such by the United States, and capable of entering into contracts and acquiring property, as well as competent, through the rule of comity, of bringing and maintaining actions in the courts of this country; but it is claimed that it does not come within the description of legal entities authorized to require security for costs. That it is within the spirit of the enactment, we think can not be disputed, and we are also of the opinion that it is within the letter as well.
>
> Vattel defines "nations or states to be bodies politic, societies of men united together for the purpose of promoting their mutual safety and advantage by the joint effort of their combined strength. Such a society has her affairs and her interests. She deliberates and takes resolutions in common, thus becoming a moral person, who possesses an understanding and a will peculiar to himself, and is susceptible of obligations and rights." (Law of Nations, 1; Wheaton's International Law, chap. 2, sec. 1, 2; Bouvier's Institutes, title "Nation.")
>
> That such a being constitutes a legal entity, capable of acquiring and enjoying property and protecting itself from injuries thereto in the courts of foreign countries, has long been recognized and established in the tribunals of civilized nations. (*Republic of Mexico* v. *De Arrangoiz*, 5 Duer, 636; *Hullet* v. *King of Spain*, 1 Dow & C., 169; *Cherokee Nation* v. *Georgia*, 5 Peters, 52.)

There can be no doubt but that under title 2, chapter 10, part 3, of the Revised Statutes, providing for security for costs in an action brought by any plaintiff, not residing within the jurisdiction of the court, that foreign states and nations were required to give such security, and we do not think that the provisions of the Code were intended to change the law in that respect.

Section 3268 of the Code is stated to be a reënactment of the previous statute, and it can not, we think, have been intended thereby to take away the right which resident defendants had to require security for costs. No reason is seen for such a change, and we do not think any was intended to be made. The word "person" was, we think, used in its enlarged sense, as comprising all legal entities except foreign corporations, which were authorized to bring actions in this state. In that sense it embraces moral persons having legal rights, capable of entering into contracts and incurring obligations, as well as natural persons. The statute must be construed with reference to the objects it had in view, the evils intended to be remedied and the benefits expected to be derived from it; and, as thus construed, we can see no reason why the plaintiff is not included within the description of persons intended to be subjected to its obligations.[1]

Conception of the Latin American State Is the Same as the North American Conception

The views which I have ventured to express concerning the origin and nature of the state, the powers which it properly exercises, and the limitations imposed upon it by the people in the act of creation, are based upon the theory and practice of the United States of America as I understand that theory and practice to be. But these views are susceptible of a much wider application. They are, I believe, applicable to all the American republics and they are shared by their publicists.

Our distinguished colleague, Mr. Alejandro Alvarez, has sketched with the hand of a master the origin and nature of the Latin American states in his monograph entitled "Chilean

---

[1]The Republic of Honduras v. Marco Aurelio Soto, 112 New York Reports, 310.

Diplomacy during the Period of Emancipation and American International Society," and I beg to invoke his authority on this point. After recounting the origin and nature of the Latin American states, and briefly but adequately sketching the origin and nature of the United States, he says:

> Although the difference between the movement of emancipation and the institutions of the United States and of Latin America are important, on the other hand there are, from a larger point of view, between both groups of countries, points in common and of the same character which give a certain unity to the American continent and differentiate it in turn from Europe.

Mr. Alvarez feels justified in thus concluding his examination of the question:

> In Europe the state is the incarnation of power and the powers of government do not have a strictly limited character.
>
> In America, inasmuch as the countries are the product of a revolutionary movement and the direct result of the popular will, it is a principle more or less expressly admitted in all constitutions that the authorities possess no greater rights than those with which they are directly invested by law.
>
> The base is individualism; that is to say, the exaltation of the individual endowed with natural rights, which he brings to society and which must be guaranteed, a conception borrowed from the political philosophers of the 17th and 18th centuries.
>
> For this reason, guarantees in favor of individuals are differently conceived. In America they have the express character of limitations of governmental action, a character which does not obtain in Europe.[1]

The American idea, in a nut-shell, is contained in the social compact of the charterless and homeless Pilgrims of the May-

---

[1] Alvarez, La Diplomacia de Chile durante la Emancipación y la Sociedad Internacional Americana, pp. 173, 176.

flower which they drafted on November 11/21, 1620, before setting foot upon American soil, and which I beg to quote:

> In the name of God, Amen. We whose names are under-written, the loyall subjects of our dread soveraigne Lord, King James, by the grace of God, of Great Britaine, Franc, and Ireland king, defender of the faith, etc., have-ing undertaken, for the glorie of God, and advancemente of the Christian faith, and honour of our king and countrie, a voyage to plant the first colonie in the North-erne parts of Virginia, doe by these presents solemnly and mutualy in the presence of God, and one of another, covenant and combine our selves togeather into a civill body politick, for our better ordering and preservation and furtherance of the ends aforesaid; and by vertue hearof to enacte, constitute, and frame such just and equall lawes, ordinances, acts, constitutions, and offices, from time to time, as shall be thought most meete and convenient for the generall good of the Colonie, unto which we promise all due submission and obedience. In witness whereof we have hereunder subscribed our names at Cap-Codd the 11. of November, in the year of the raigne of our soveraigne lord, King James, of England, France, and Ireland the eighteenth, and of Scotland the fiftie fourth. An°: Dom. 1620.[1]

With these pregnant words ringing in our ears we can un-derstand what the poet Lowell meant when he spoke of the Pilgrim fathers as "stern men, with empires in their brains." For, if we eliminate the expression "the loyall subjects of our dread soveraigne Lord, King James," the Declaration of Inde-pendence is already here as the acorn, needing only congenial soil for the sturdy oak.

It is unnecessary for present purposes to examine further the question of the origin of the American state or its nature, as my purpose is merely to make clear that the state, at least in the American conception, is a creature of law and is subor-dinated to the law of its creation.

If this is true of one state, it must be true of other states.

---

[1] Bradford's History of Plymouth Plantation, edited by W. T. Davis, 1908, p. 107.

It is certainly true of the American states, and, assuming
that Chief Judge Ruger's decision in the case of *Honduras* v.
de Soto is correct, it follows that it is true of all states.   International law speaks no uncertain language in this connection, and the authorities are at one in considering a state
from the point of view of law to be a moral or artificial person, body politic or corporation. Assuming the correctness of
Aristotle's view that men are associated in political society and
that the unit of political society in international law is a state,
it follows that, if there be a society of states or of nations, it is
a society of political entities, each one of which is independent
of the other and is the equal of each or all, according to the
philosophy of the Declaration of Independence, because we can
not claim a right for our own state which we deny to any other.

There Must Be, Therefore There Is a Society of States or Nations

We do not need to speculate whether the states, like individuals, would, if left to themselves, form a society. It would
seem, however, that Aristotle's reasoning in this matter is
susceptible of a larger application, because, if men form societies by virtue of a social instinct, and political societies,
which we call bodies politic, because they are as he says
political animals, it would follow that, all states being composed of men of the social and political instincts attributed
to them by Aristotle, the societies which they have made
would themselves tend to form a larger society. The language of Aristotle is so interesting that I beg to quote it. "A
social instinct," he says, "is implanted in all men by nature,"
by virtue of which they form society, and "that man is by
nature a political animal," by virtue whereof he forms political society.

There Must Be and There Is, a Solidarity of Nations as Recognized by the Hague Peace Conferences

It is not necessary, however, to rest the existence of the
society of nations upon Aristotle, although the application of

the social and political instinct with which he invests man would tend to justify the contention that a society of states or of nations would come into being. I do not need to argue the matter, as the states themselves have by their accredited representatives on a very solemn occasion within the past decade confirmed their solemn act recognizing the existence of such a society. Thus, in the preamble to the convention of 1899 for the pacific settlement of international disputes, the representatives of twenty-six nations in conference at The Hague spoke of their governments as "recognizing the solidarity which unites the members of the society of civilized nations," and, in 1907, the representatives of forty-four nations, likewise assembled in conference at The Hague, confirmed this statement.

Nor do I need to prove that the advantages of the society of nations are so great that it must needs come into being; because it is in being and its existence is certified by the official act of forty-four states. It is to be observed, however, that the society spoken of is the society of civilized states, and that the representatives of the forty-four states recognized the solidarity uniting the members of the society.

Whether or not the views which I have put forward as to the nature of the state be contested by European publicists, it is a fact they are not contested by American publicists, so that we have twenty-one states, one less than half of all those participating in the second Hague Peace Conference, recognizing this doctrine of the origin and of the nature of the state, and they necessarily recognize at one and the same time their own solidarity when they recognize the solidarity of the states forming the society of civilized nations. If this conception of the nature of the state, common to American publicists, be not accepted by the world at large, it is nevertheless a consolation to us to know that it is and must be accepted by the twenty-one American republics, for we know that a doctrine accepted by these twenty-one states has a fair chance to become universal. In any event, it is continental, and the doctrine of a continent can not be disrespectfully treated.

The Hague Peace Conference has thus solemnly spoken on two occasions of the solidarity which unites the members of the society of civilized nations. And if this solidarity exists between and among the most distant and diverse members of the society of nations it is reasonable to expect that solidarity would exist in a more marked degree between and among nations which are to one another as neighbors, and whose antecedents and institutions are similar if not identical. We would expect an American solidarity, and the expectation is borne out by the facts.

The Solidarity of Nations is an American Doctrine and is Most Marked Among the Republics of the American Continent.

Speaking in the first instance of the English colonies of North America, it is common knowledge that like origin, like traditions, like language, like institutions and a common grievance brought them together for a redress of this grievance and held them together after it had been redressed by independence. The solidarity here was so deep rooted that it resulted in the legislative, administrative and judicial union which we call the United States of America. Had the solidarity which drew the colonies inevitably into oneness been less evident and the causes more remote, the states might have maintained their independence of one another while recognizing their common interest to defend themselves against the foreigner.

This is what has happened in Latin America, where federation has been suggested although not effected, but where a solidarity exists which causes the foreigner to look upon them as if they were one; drawn together by common origin, by a common language and by common traditions, they are, as it were, many states but one people. They are the product of revolution, just as the United States is the product of revolution; the likeness of origin and the similarity, not to say identity of institutions, reënforced by geographical position, have brought them together, so that there exists an American solidarity not merely like that recognized by The Hague but a solidarity which is a name and an institution.

Pan Americanism is a fact, although its opponents would call it a sentiment, as if a sentiment were not a fact, and it has as its outward and visible sign of a spiritual and inward grace the Pan American Union, composed of the twenty-one American republics.

I would like to dwell a moment upon Pan American solidarity, and lest I should seem to give a freer rein to imagination than to facts let me quote several passages from the authoritative and charming study, which I have already laid under contribution, of our distinguished colleague, Alejandro Alvarez. Thus he says:

> The notion of solidarity is essentially American and had its most brilliant manifestations in the struggle of the Spanish colonies of this continent for their emancipation. . . . This solidarity was nothing else than a sentiment of mutual affection among all of the colonies, based upon a community of origin and of destiny.
>
> Under Spanish domination they were united by intimate bonds of fraternity, the result of identity of blood, language, religion, education, legislation and customs, and the fact of a common submission under a like colonial régime.
>
> But in that epoch this sentiment did not find a noticeable expression. It was only when a foreign danger menaced them and the movement of emancipation began to take form that the colonists realized they had a common cause to defend.[1]

In another passage of his work, the same distinguished publicist says:

> Without the largeness of view that this continental solidarity gave to the struggle, without the energy and the generous warmth which this ideal communicated to the spirit, it would have assuredly been impossible for Latin America to obtain its independence at the time in which it did.[2]

---

[1]Alvarez, La Diplomacia de Chile durante la Emancipación y la Sociedad Internacional Americana, pp. 57–8.

[2]Ibid., p. 61.

A little later in the course of his narrative, Mr. Alvarez traces the growth of a continental solidarity as distinct from that of the Spanish American states.

> This solidarity thereafter took a new direction, charac-terized by the representations made by the United States before the European courts to obtain their recognition of the sovereignty of these countries, and by the recognition which the Government of the United States itself has-tened to make. The proclamation of the Monroe Doctrine came to the aid and strengthened the sentiment, combin-ing in a happy formula the ideas of the American nations concerning their right to preserve their independence and to oppose the attempts of the European states to oppress, to reconquer, or to colonize any part of their territory.
>
> Pan American solidarity, therefore, came into existence at one and the same time with Spanish American solidar-ity, but before Latin American solidarity, which would also include Brazil. This last continental tie only came into being during the second half of the nineteenth cen-tury, based upon the likeness of the political and interna-tional problems of Brazil to those of the other Latin American states of the new continent.[1]
>
> Likewise in the period of emancipation there were writ-ers and statesmen who foresaw the larger and more last-ing solidarity which should make itself felt not only in periods of struggle but also in the normal life of the peo-ples of the American continent, giving form to their mu-tual relations and coöperating in their growth and prog-ress. That is to say, they foresaw and they desired to organize a real American international society, which by the unity of its views, its subordination to law and its peaceful tendencies stood in marked contrast with the in-ternational European community, which at that time was constantly engaged in recurring struggles for domination.[2]

Let me conclude this brief statement of American solidarity with another quotation from Mr. Alvarez, in which he points out the influence of similarity of institutions upon solidarity.

---

[1] *Ibid.*, pp. 66-7.
[2] *Ibid.*, pp. 82-3.

The similarity of this system among the Latin American states and between them and the United States reënforced the sentiment of solidarity among all of them, with the result that the international American society clothed itself with a character different from that of Europe.[1]

As a citizen of the English-speaking Republic I have hesitated to speak of the solidarity which I hope and believe exists between the twenty Latin American countries and the Republic of the North. I felt that you would prefer a statement of American solidarity, if it were to be made, to come from a Latin American source, and I have therefore drawn upon the admirable statement of American solidarity made by Mr. Alvarez, with whom Pan Americanism is at once a religion and a reality.

For the purposes of the American Institute, dealing with American problems, we can accept the American doctrine of the origin and nature of the state and, without seeking further to demonstrate the solidarity which unites the American republics, we need only point to the Pan American Union, with its governing board in Washington, composed of a duly appointed and accredited member of each of the American republics, in order to establish the existence of a very marked and special solidarity uniting the members of the American continent.

The Society of Nations Needs Law and Therefore a Law of the Society Exists

I have been anxious to consider the American state from the point of view of its founders, to establish the existence of the society of nations and within that society a smaller group, if necessary, composed of the twenty-one American republics, recognizing the American conception of the state, because I want to show in the next place that there is and must be a law of that society just as there is and must be a law for any society.

---

[1] *Ibid.*, p. 177.

It is true that in this matter I am dealing again with truisms, but, if all persons and nations professing truisms practiced them, law and order instead of anarchy would exist between nations and we would not be meeting at this moment in the midst of a world war, which threatens the existence of the society of nations and which jeopardizes civilization.

I might perhaps quote Aristotle on the question of law and prove its need by his apt illustration of law even among robbers, but I shall content myself with the happier expression of Cicero: *Ubi societas, ibi jus*—"where there is society, there is law." Where men come together and form society, they agree upon certain rules of conduct, prescribing the rights of the members and the duties of each toward one and all. No matter how small the society may be, there must be some rules regulating admission to it, otherwise, it is open to all who care to enter, and, unless there be rules of conduct agreed upon, there may be at any time confusion and anarchy. Whether the purpose of the society be scientific, social or political, the need of a rule of conduct to control and to guide its members is obvious, and the experience of mankind has shown how necessary and wholly indispensable such rules of conduct are in political society.

Within each and every nation laws exist prescribing the rights and duties of the citizens or subjects making up the state, and these rules or laws taken together constitute what is called national law. An examination of the systems of law of the different nations shows that there are some principles everywhere prevailing. As they are to be found everywhere in modern civilized society, they can be called universal, and, being universal they may likewise be termed fundamental. These principles are (1) the right to life, (2) the right to liberty, (3) the right to the pursuit of happiness, as proclaimed by the Declaration of Independence of the United States, (4) the right to legal equality, (5) the right to property, and (6) the right to the enjoyment of all these rights. This is a very brief and very summary statement of a very

long process, for the rights thus enumerated within the compass of a single sentence have been the slow and almost inper-
ceptible growth of centuries. It would be historically false to assert that upon them the system of national law has been reared.
They are rather the half dozen principles to be deduced from
the municipal codes, which exist in the countries which, taken
together, make up the society of nations. But if these provisions which I venture to call universal and fundamental are to
be taken as the culmination of development and as the résumé
of the different systems, it follows that from them we could
derive the various provisions of the different municipal codes
if the codes were not in existence. We can not claim, as
I have already said, that these principles, historically considered, are the foundations upon which the municipal codes
have been based, but we are justified analytically, though not
historically, in maintaining that they are at the present day, as
the result of a long and painful period of development, to be
considered as the foundations upon which the municipal systems of law securely rest. Admitting that these principles have
been the result of long and painful growth, the question arises
is it necessary that we shall go through the same processes in
developing international law? Must we repeat on an international scale what has been done in every country and therefore
done upon the largest of possible scales? Can we not regard
these principles as already established, without the necessity of
going through the process of their development and upon them
as established build the law which is to obtain between and
among nations? We are asking nothing new of the nations.
We are not suggesting that they take a leap in the dark or
that they pledge themselves to accept the unknown, for these
principles, existing in every nation, are familiar to the people
of each nation. They are therefore familiar to all persons
who, grouped artificially in states, make up the world, or, at
least, that part of it which we call the society of nations.

To accomplish this we need only ask that those principles
which are applied within each group and which are thus com-

mon to all, shall be held to apply between and among the peoples of the different groups, just as they apply between and among the persons of each and every group considered as a separate and distinct unit. From this viewpoint, the only difficulty in the way is to persuade the nations that these fundamental principles can be accepted and applied by them in their mutual relations; but, as the very principles in question have already been accepted by their subjects and citizens, there should be no insuperable barrier in the way to prevent them from regulating the conduct of nations, if only what I have ventured to call the American conception of the state be adopted.

Although I have already urged this conception upon you, let me nevertheless repeat it in this connection, as it is very material to my argument. The American conception, as I understand it and as I advocate it, is that the state is a moral, juristic or artificial person, a body politic or a corporation; that the state thus conceived is a creature of the popular will, subjected to and subordinated to the law of its creation; that it is a mere creation of the people, a mere agency of the people, the servant of the people, to carry into effect the purposes stated in the Declaration of Independence, with a form of government most likely to effect the safety and happiness of the people creating the state and devising the form of government. From this point of view, the state is not something mystical, superhuman and of divine origin, nor is its form of government created to meet the desires of a class or of a privileged few or of a sanctified and glorified family.

But before we can make any progress in the direction which I have indicated, we must ask ourselves whether the fundamental conceptions of municipal law are capable of being translated into terms of international law, and if, when so translated, they can serve as the foundation upon which an adequate and progressive law of nations may be built. It seems to me that each one of these principles which I have ventured to term fundamental can be internationalized and applied to the relations of nations. The right to life, stated in terms of international law, is the right of the state to exist and to maintain its existence. The right to liberty is the right of the state to develop itself without hindrance from without, that is to say, to be independent of the control or supervision of another state. The right to the pursuit of happiness is, in terms of international law, the right to pursue that conduct best fitted to the state and which when pursued makes for the happiness of its people. The right to legal equality—the Declaration of Independence proclaims that all men are created equal—means in municipal law not that every person is equal in capacity or in ability, but that every person has the same rights and duties in law and under law, a right which in terms of international law means that every state, be it large or small, rich or poor, is a juristic person and as such the equal of every other juristic person which we call a state or nation. The right to property, everywhere existent in municipal law, expressed in terms of international law, means the right of the state to have and to hold territory within defined boundaries and to exercise within its boundaries exclusive jurisdiction. And, finally, the right to the enjoyment of these various rights exists in international law as well as in municipal law, because, if rights are not to be enjoyed they are useless.

At the same time, it will not have escaped attention that each right raises a duty, for, if I have a right to my life, everybody is bound to respect this right, otherwise it is to me of no avail. Every right on the part of one person is accompanied by a duty on the part of all persons to observe it, and on the part of the government, instituted by the people forming the state, to protect this right and to protect me in its enjoyment.

Now, I have been bold enough to say that these are the fundamental rights of municipal law and of every state belonging to the society of nations, and I am bold enough to assert that they are likewise the fundamental rights of every state considered as a member of the society of nations. I believe that they are the foundation of the law of nations just as they are the foundation of the law of each nation, and that, just as the provisions of the municipal law can be developed from them, so the provisions of international law can be developed from them, and indeed that the provisions of international law must be developed from them, if we are to have law instead of anarchy in the society of nations. We may readily admit this to be true in much the same way as we say that two and two make four, without stopping to draw the consequences from the admission. We look upon these principles as true only in the abstract, not as applicable to the relations of nations; yet if we accept them we must insist that they be applied between nations. Otherwise it is useless to descant about them.

I do not intend at this time to dwell longer upon this subject, as, during the course of this session of the Institute, I shall present a project dealing with the rights and duties of nations, based upon the fundamental rights of municipal law, and I shall accompany the declaration with a commentary showing that each one of these principles is not merely true in municipal law, but that each is true in international law; that these principles have not merely been devised by philosophers and expounded in treatises on the science, but that they have been authoritatively stated, and applied by the Supreme Court of the United States in cases involving them, and that they are accepted as thus defined and applied by every republic of the western world.

But I can not resist the temptation to reënforce, by a semblance of authority, the statements which I have felt justified in making, and indeed I feel that I might properly expose myself to criticism if I did not, however briefly and inadequately, put you in possession of these authorities, in order that you may here and now test the accuracy of my conclusions and be in a position to accept, to reject, or to modify the declaration of rights and duties when its text is laid before you. In the language of the Declaration of Independence, "let facts be submitted to a candid world."

In the first place, and by way of introduction, I beg to quote the language of a distinguished North American jurist, peculiarly versed in what may be called comparative jurisprudence. In his "Modern Political Institutions," published well-nigh twenty years ago, the Honorable Simeon E. Baldwin, who is the presiding officer of the subsection of public law in the present Scientific Congress, said:

> The principles of jurisprudence, also, recognized as governing the relations of private citizens to each other, are substantially the same in all the leading nations of the world; and they are the same because they are derived from the conception of the equality of right.[1]

The Half Dozen Fundamental Principles of Law for the Society of Nations as Stated and Defined by the Supreme Court of the United States.

Let me now take up the fundamental principles of municipal law which I have sought to express in terms of international law. In the first place, I have stated that the right to life, everywhere recognized in municipal law, is in the law of nations the right of the state to exist and to maintain its existence. On this point I beg to call your attention to two cases, one American, the other English, which, taken together, state the nature and extent of the right and its necessary limitation.

Thus, in the Chinese Exclusion case, decided by the Supreme Court of the United States in 1888, it was expressly stated:

> To preserve its independence, and give security against foreign aggression and encroachment, is the highest duty of every nation, and to attain these ends nearly all other considerations are to be subordinated.

You will observe that the court was careful to limit the right

---

[1]Baldwin's Modern Political Institutions, 1898, p. 341.

which it claimed by the use of the expression "nearly." Otherwise, necessity, that is to say, alleged necessity, might override law.

The English case is entitled *Regina* v. *Dudley*, decided by the Queen's Bench Division of the High Court of Justice in 1884.[1] It held, in effect, that it was unlawful for shipwrecked sailors to take the life of one of their number in order to preserve their own lives, because it was unlawful, according to the common law of England, for an English subject to take human life unless in self defense against the unlawful attack of an assailant threatening the life of the party unlawfully attacked. It is true that this was a case of private law, but it is, in my opinion, equally applicable to the artificial as well as to the natural person. The plea advanced in this case was the plea of necessity, but after an elaborate examination of this defense the court very properly rejected it. In the course of his opinion, Lord Chief Justice Coleridge, who had had large experience in public affairs and, as Attorney General had been the adviser to his Government in international as well as in municipal law, made some statements which deserve quotation. Thus, he said:

> Now it is admitted that the deliberate killing of this unoffending and unresisting boy was clearly murder, unless the killing can be justified by some well-recognized excuse admitted by the law. It is further admitted that there was in this case no such excuse, unless the killing was justified by what has been called necessity. But the temptation to the act which existed here was not what the law has ever called necessity. Nor is this to be regretted. Though law and morality are not the same, and though many things may be immoral which are not necessarily illegal, yet the absolute divorce of law from morality would be of fatal consequence, and such divorce would follow if the temptation to murder in this case were to be held by law an absolute defense of it. It is

---

[1]Reported in 15 Cox's Criminal Cases, p. 624; 14 Queen's Bench Division, p. 273.

not so. To preserve one's life is, generally speaking, a duty; but it may be the plainest and highest duty to sacrifice it. War is full of instances in which it is a man's duty not to live but to die.

After having rejected the plea of necessity, the Lord Chief Justice points out the consequences of its admission in the following passage:

It is not needful to point out the awful danger of admitting the principle which has been contended for. Who is to be the judge of this sort of necessity? By what measure is the comparative value of lives to be measured? Is it to be strength, or intellect, or what? It is plain that the principle leaves to him who is to profit by it to determine the necessity which will justify him in deliberately taking another's life to save his own. In this case the weakest, the youngest, the most unresisting was chosen. Was it more necessary to kill him than one of the grown men? The answer must be, No.
"So spake the Fiend, and with necessity,
The tyrant's plea, excused his devilish deeds."

The right to liberty, which in terms of international law is the right of the state to develop itself and to be independent of the control or supervision of any other state, and the right of equality are so closely related, indeed they are interrelated, that they may be considered together as different phases of one and the same right, and they are in fact so treated by the authorities. Thus, Sir William Scott, later Lord Stowell, said, in the case of *The Louis*, decided in 1817.[1]

Two principles of public law are generally recognized as fundamental. One is the perfect equality and entire independence of all distinct states. Relative magnitude creates no distinction of right; relative imbecility, whether permanent or casual, gives no additional right to the more powerful neighbor; and any advantage seized upon that ground is mere usurpation. This is the great foundation

[1] Reported in 2 Dodson's Reports, pp. 210, 243-44.

of public law, which it mainly concerns the peace of mankind, both in their politic and private capacities, to preserve inviolate.

The Supreme Court of the United States is no less outspoken. Thus, the great Chief Justice of the United States, John Marshall, said in the case of the *Antelope,* decided in 1825:[1]

> No principle of general law is more universally acknowledged than the perfect equality of nations. Russia and Geneva have equal rights. It results from this equality, that no one can rightfully impose a rule on another. Each legislates for itself, but its legislation can operate on itself alone. . . . As no nation can prescribe a rule for others, none can make a law of nations.

It would seem that these two cases, decided by the greatest judges in matters international which the English-speaking countries have produced, settle beyond the fear of contradiction the right of a nation to the pursuit of happiness and to be considered as the equal of all other countries.

I shall ask your indulgence, however, while I dwell somewhat upon the question of equality, inasmuch as we hear it constantly asserted that it is a mere phrase, designed to tickle the ear of the small states, but that it is unthinkable that great nations should seriously consider applying it in their relations with the smaller states. The lion and the lamb, we are told, can not lie down together. As a concession, equality is recognized in strictly legal relations, for the advocates of superiority admit that in courts of justice, although nowhere else, the great and the little may stand together for a moment upon an equality. It is unknown in political as distinct from legal relations. Indeed it is bad form even to suggest it in society.

That equality has been a hope and goal, rather than a reality and a practice, may be admitted, but if the conception of the state which I have laid before you be correct, and if the theory

---

[1] 10 Wheaton's Reports, pp. 66, 122.

and practice of the United States be worthy of notice, it will be evident that equality is not the strange, uncouth, unknown and impossible thing which the superciliousness and boundless arrogance of the larger states would have us imagine.

If a state be a body politic, a corporation, a creature of the law rather than of the imagination, and an agent of the people rather than an agent of the monarch's divine right to govern wrong, it will require more obtuseness on the part of the large states to misconceive this conception and to reject it in the future than we are justified in imputing to them or their rulers. For if a state be a body politic, it must have the same rights and duties before and under the law, although the influence of one state may be greater than that of another. "There is one glory of the sun, and another glory of the moon, and another glory of the stars: for one star differeth from another star in glory."

There is, however, something to be said even for political equality, as distinct from legal or juridical equality, and the United States has said it. In the Constitutional Convention which met in Philadelphia in 1787, the advocates of the big states proposed, as is the wont of such, to ride rough-shod over the little ones. The government which they proposed was to be one in which they should, so to speak, hold the whip-hand, and the little states were to deem themselves fortunate to be permitted to enjoy the pleasures and the advantages of the company of their betters.

But there was a lion in the way. The little states were more numerous than the large ones, just as in this world of ours the poor are more numerous than their supposed betters, although, as President Lincoln has said, "God must like the common people, or he would not have made so many of them." The little states unexpectedly refused to cut off their own heads. They were unwilling to enter a union—and membership was to be voluntary—in which their rights, political as well as legal, were not to be the same. The large states proposed that a Congress, consisting of two chambers, should be composed of delegates or representatives, all chosen according to the population of each state, giving the populous states larger representation and enabling them to outvote the less populous states.[1] But the people of the small states considered that they were as good as the people of the large states; that in the Revolution, which had so happily resulted in their independence, they had staked their lives, their liberties and their property just as the large states had done; that they all were sovereign and equal states, and that in the final adjustment they should be recognized and treated as equals. They therefore proposed that the states should be equally represented.[2] The result was a compromise:[3] a Congress consisting of two houses—the Senate, to be composed of two members from each state, and the House of Representatives, to be chosen upon a basis of population from the different states. The first article of the Constitution thus states this fundamental and beneficent compromise:

> All legislative powers herein granted shall be vested in the Congress of the United States, which shall consist of a Senate and House of Representatives.
> The Senate of the United States shall be composed of two senators from each state, chosen by the legislature thereof for six years, and each Senator shall have one vote.
> The House of Representatives shall be composed of members chosen every second year by the people of the several states, and the electors in each state shall have the qualifications requisite for the electors of the most numerous branch of the state legislature.

In order that the states as they existed should not be dismembered or deprived of their equal representation in the Senate, it was further provided in the Constitution that new states should not "be formed or erected within the jurisdic-

---

[1]Farrand: The Records of the Federal Convention, 1911, vol. I, p. 228.
[2]*Ibid.*, pp. 241, 242.
[3]*Ibid.*, pp. 523, 526.

tion of another state; nor any state be formed by the junction of two or more states or parts of states, without the consent of the legislature in the states concerned as well as of the Congress," and as far as representation was concerned, "that no state, without its consent, shall be deprived of its equal suffrage in the Senate."

The fears of critics of democratic government seem in large measure to be that democracy, meaning thereby the many rather than the minority, will make law where they can not make right, and that we are in the danger of substituting the tyranny of the many for the tyranny of the few or of the one. It is to be observed that this criticism can be met and indeed has been met in the American system by the majority consciously imposing a restraint upon themselves in the exercise of what they declare to be their rights, for, while the American people reserve the right to amend their Constitution and can at any moment resume the power which they granted in the Constitutional Convention in 1787, they nevertheless made the exercise of the right to amend the Constitution depend upon more than the will of a majority of the Congress or of the state or of the people within the states. Thus, Article V of the Constitution, dealing with this question, which has been called the keystone of the Federal fabric, provides:

> The Congress, whenever two-thirds of both Houses shall deem it necessary, shall propose Amendments to this Constitution, or, on the Application of the Legislatures of two-thirds of the several States, shall call a Convention for proposing Amendments, which, in either Case, shall be valid to all Intents and Purposes, as Part of this Constitution, when ratified by the Legislatures of three-fourths of the several States, or by Conventions in three fourths thereof, as the one or the other Mode of Ratification may be proposed by the Congress.

This is the problem in a nutshell and this is the solution. Restraint imposed from above or from without is tyranny or despotism. Restraint imposed from within is self-restraint, and is liberty.

In the teeth of this history and in view of the fundamental provisions of the law of the land, it is difficult to see how a North American with a knowledge of one and a respect for the other can object to equality, whether it be political or legal.

The right to property, recognized alike in municipal and in international law, means in this latter system, as I already have said, the right of a state to hold territory within defined boundaries and to exercise exclusive jurisdiction in such territory. The theory of the nature and extent of this right is admirably stated, if I may say so, by Mr. Chief Justice Marshall in the following passages from his judgment in the case of the schooner *Exchange,* decided in 1812:[1]

> The jurisdiction of the nation, within its own territory, is necessarily exclusive and absolute; it is susceptible of no limitation, not imposed by itself. Any restriction upon it, deriving validity from an external source, would imply a diminution of its sovereignty, to the extent of the restriction, and an investment of that sovereignty, to the same extent, in that power which could impose such restriction. All exceptions, therefore, to the full and complete power of a nation, within its own territories, must be traced up to the consent of the nation itself. They can flow from no other legitimate source.

The great Chief Justice, however, recognized that *summum jus* is often *summa injuria,* and he therefore qualified the extreme right by the existence of a duty. Thus:

> A nation would justly be considered as violating its faith, although that faith might not be expressly plighted, which should suddenly and without previous notice, exercise its territorial powers in a manner not consonant to the usages and received obligations of the civilized world.

[1] 7 Cranch's Reports, pp. 116, 136-7.

This duty he bases upon the common interest of equal and independent nations. Thus:

> This perfect equality and absolute independence of sovereigns, and this common interest impelling them to mutual intercourse, and an interchange of good offices with each other, have given rise to a class of cases in which every sovereign is understood to waive the exercise of a part of that complete exclusive territorial jurisdiction, which has been stated to be the attribute of every nation.

I have frequently remarked that rights would be worthless things if they did not carry with them the duty of observance. This principle is fundamental because, without it, the rights which I have enumerated might exist in theory, but they could not exist in fact. We could establish by argument the right to enjoyment and the duty of observance; but fortunately we do not need to do so, as the Supreme Court of the United States has anticipated our needs and has supplied us with the authority, going even further than we could ask, by making it the duty of each and every state not merely to recognize the rights of others but to protect the rights thus recognized.

In the case of *United States* v. *Arjona,* decided in 1886,[1] Mr. Chief Justice Waite, peculiarly qualified by his large experience in public affairs—for had he not represented the United States before the Geneva Tribunal of Arbitration—said for the court:

> But if the United States can require this of another, that other may require it of them, because international obligations are of necessity reciprocal in their nature. The right, if it exists at all, is given by the law of nations, and what is law for one is, under the same circumstances, law for the other. A right secured by the law of nations to a nation, or its people, is one the United

---

[1] 120 U. S. Reports, pp. 479, 487.

States as the representatives of this nation are bound to protect.

I am very anxious to have these matters considered and to have the Institute define its attitude toward them, because we must affirm our faith in these as the fundamental principles of international law upon which the new law of nations must be built. When almost every dispatch from the old world announces some new violation of international law, when even its votaries lose courage and fear the destruction of the system, it becomes us and it behooves us publicly as individuals and as an organized Institute to confess our faith in international law as a system of justice and as a branch of jurisprudence, and upon the principles of justice and in accordance with the methods of jurisprudence to contribute, as best we may, to the upbuilding of that law which must exist between nations.

In no uncertain measure, the future of international law is with the Americas. If a great English statesman could boast that he had called the new world into existence to redress the balance of the old, let it be our claim to remembrance that the Americas, rejecting the balance of power, shall redress the misfortunes of the old world, by incorporating in the law of nations those principles of justice which have produced and maintained law and order, peace and content wherever they have existed and whenever they have been applied.

The Society of Nations Needs and Therefore has a Law-Making Body in the Hague Peace Conference

I am well aware that international law will not grow of itself, and that, as within nations the legislature steps in and by statute accelerates the growth of custom, so in the society of nations there must be some organ which will quicken the development of international law.

We must not, however, confuse the nation with the society of nations. We must recognize that the very close union within national boundaries does not exist in the society of nations, that, while persons living within the nation may create a legislature and invest it with the power to command, it is difficult if not impossible to create a legislature and invest it with power over nations regarding themselves as sovereign, independent and equal.   But is it necessary that we should carry over into the international field the agencies and instrumentalities of national life without changing and fitting them to the conditions of the new environment?   We may profit by the experience of nations, and if national agencies and instrumentalities have justified themselves on a small scale and within a modest domain, may we not hope that they will render like services upon a larger scale and within the international field?   But, given the difference of conditions, we should expect a difference in the institutions.   If it is feasible to create a legislature within the nation, to endow it with the powers of a superior power and to invest its will with the force of law, we should, recognizing the difference of conditions in the international field, expect that a conference instead of a legislature should meet; that in this conference the states should be represented upon a plane of equality; that its resolutions should not have the force of law, but that they should be recommendations of the Conference to the different states, to adopt and to ratify, and, in so doing, to make them law.

Fortunately, a wise and enlightened monarch had in 1898 the vision to call a conference which met at The Hague, to consider matters of importance to the world at large and to take action in the interest not of one power, but of all powers. This Conference met in 1899 in The Hague and is known as the First Hague Peace Conference. A second was called and met in 1907 in the same quiet and stately city.   The first was composed of representatives from twenty-six states, the second of representatives from forty-four nations.   The first sat from the middle of May until the end of July, the second from the middle of June until the middle of October, thereby demonstrating that not merely twenty-six, but that forty-four nations could meet in conference, not only for the period of two months, but for the period of four months, not merely to consider matters of advantage to one power, but those of advantage to all nations of varying degrees of civilization. These conferences drafted conventions and declarations. They were signed by the representatives of the powers, and they were then transmitted to the participating nations by the Netherland Government, acting in behalf of the Conference. They have been ratified by the appropriate branches of the national governments and the ratifications have been deposited at The Hague. In fact, a law-making body has made its appearance in the society of nations, not in the form of a legislature, which imposes its will and prevails by physical force, but in the simpler guise of a conference, which recommends and prevails by the wisdom and reasonableness of its projects. This institution is fitted to the needs of the society of nations. If it should meet at stated periods, and be given a definite organization and a procedure acceptable to the participants, the society of nations would have its organ for the development of law, without which anarchy must prevail, as it prevails today, but with which justice would be extended and would prevail in the uttermost corners of the earth.

I dare not go into further details. I must content myself with this passing notice, but I have felt it to be my duty to point out that a law-making organ is in existence or may be brought into being, consistent with the sovereignty, independence and equality of the members of the society of nations. The nations have recognized their solidarity; they only need to give effect to its recognition.

The American Institute can not devote itself to a more important subject. The society of nations exists, based upon civilization and a recognition of the solidarity of civilized states. The society of nations must become conscious of its existence and must endow itself with the agencies and instrumentalities necessary for its preservation and for the preservation of each of its members, without sacrificing the sovereignty, the independence and the equality of any. The Hague Conference is the key to unlock these difficulties. I feel keenly that the Institute should first pronounce itself upon the fundamentals of international law and that it should next express itself as to the best means of developing international law through periodical conferences of the nations, meeting at stated intervals. I would suggest that at the second session of the Institute this matter be considered, and I shall take the liberty of presenting a project at this meeting which, without any claim to finality or of solving or indeed of meeting the difficulties, may nevertheless serve as the basis of discussion and as an incentive to other and better projects.

The Society of Nations Needs a Court and Therefore it Will Have One to Ascertain and to Apply the Principles of Justice to Disputes Among its Members.

Admitting, as indeed we must admit, that there is a society of nations, that this society, like each and every other society, must have its law, that it must have its agency for the development of its law, I desire in conclusion to offer some observations upon the necessity of having an agency to ascertain this law and to apply it to the disputes or differences which must arise in any society, and which from a sad and a secular experience we know occur in the society of nations and disturb its peace and quiet.

It would perhaps be too much to say that it is useless to have law if it be not applied, because its very existence suggests its application. But it rarely happens that any law is so clear and unmistakable as not to give rise to a difference of meaning and to require an authoritative interpretation, and we know from our own experience, that, when great interests are involved, we cling to the letter of the law, if it be in our favor, and that we invoke the spirit if the letter killeth. We can not safely be entrusted with the interpretation of a law involving our rights. It may be a sad commentary upon human nature, but it is human nature and this being so we should admit it, recognize it, and provide against it. We can not escape human nature; we can not escape ourselves; we can not escape history. The laws of every society must be interpreted, if the rights and duties of its members are to be ascertained and enforced. Every state belonging to the society of nations recognizes this, for every state has courts to ascertain the law, to interpret it, and to apply it in the disputes which arise between its citizens or subjects. There is not a single state making pretense to civilization and progress in which such agencies are lacking, and yet the society of nations, the greatest and the most impressive of all, has no agency to ascertain its law, to interpret it, and to apply it to the disputes which must necessarily occur between them by virtue of their contact and which will become more numerous as the nations are more closely brought into contact.

Now, if we find certain principles of law to obtain universally we may consider them as fundamental. If we find the method of development of law to be by legislature in every country, we can consider this method fundamental; and if we find some agency for the ascertainment of a rule of law and its application to disputes that may arise between and among citizens and subjects of every country, we are justified in believing that such an agency is fundamental. We are met, therefore, in any examination of national organization, be it superficial or profound, with three great universal, fundamental facts: the fact of law, the fact of law-making bodies, and the fact of law-administering bodies; and, if we find these facts everywhere existing in the state or existing in every state, we are justified, indeed, we are driven inevitably to the conclusion that these facts are fundamental facts of political society; that they are requisite to the maintenance of political society, if they are not inherent in its nature, and that we would expect to find them, albeit perhaps in rudimentary form, in early society, indeed in any society aware of its existence and properly organized.

Let me quote, without again commenting upon it, a passage from Aristotle's politics—true when he wrote it, true today, true of all conceivable time: "A social instinct is implanted in all men by nature, and yet he who first founded the state was the greatest of benefactors. For man, when perfected, is the best of animals, but, when separated from law and justice, he is the worst of all; since armed injustice is the more dangerous, and he is equipped at birth with the arms of intelligence and with moral qualities which he may use for the worst ends. Wherefore, if he have not virtue, he is the most unholy and the most savage of animals, and the most full of lust and gluttony. But justice is the bond of men in states, and the administration of justice, which is the determination of what is just, is the principle of order in political society."

Admitting that the administration of justice is the principle or order in political society, we must have agencies for its administration. But, in the first place, we must needs determine what is just. Now, our daily experience must have convinced us that high-minded and honest men, although they may agree in general as to what is just in the abstract, differ as to what is just in the concrete case, especially if they be personally affected by the case. A community can not be torn asunder. It must act as a unit, and it can only do so if it has ideas in common, that is to say, if fundamental ideas are held and shared in common. What the community needs is, not that the ideas of a select few shall prevail, but that there shall be a general agreement concerning these matters. We may admit that the ideas of enlightened men concerning justice are preferable to those of the unlettered, although this question is by no means free from doubt and history has much to say in favor of the many as against the few. The conception of justice to prevail in the community must be the ideas of justice held by people generally in the community if these ideas of justice are to prevail. Instead of the individual sense, which made itself known and was rejected in self-redress, we have the community sense of justice. This community sense, although it may not be so high and so theoretically perfect as the sense of the enlightened few, sets the standard and the test of conduct within the community, and as the standard of the many it has the better chance of being obeyed.

Whenever it is necessary, society determines for itself and prescribes for all what is just by statute, instead of leaving it to slow-footed custom. And not content to determine and to prescribe what is just, when the need arises, it determines and prescribes it in advance, so that it may be known of all men, so that it may not seem to be the result of a particular case in which the disputants are interested, so that it may be justice alike in the abstract and in the concrete case.

Although justice is general, we may expect the rules of justice to vary from time to time, because a rule of conduct is often a matter of expediency. Justice as such is a matter of right and the progress of mankind consists in the transfer of justice from the abstract to the concrete through rules of law. But the experience of mankind shows that two agencies are needed in this matter: one agency to determine what is just in general and to make rules of law in accordance with the conception of justice obtaining in the community; and another agency to determine what is just in the particular case, that is to say, to pick out, or by analogy to frame in accordance with general principles, the rule applicable to the concrete case. One body is the legislature, the other is the court.

If justice is the bond of men in states, if the administration of justice is the determination of what is just, and if justice is the principle of order in political society, it behooves us to strengthen the bond between men by increasing their sense of and belief in justice, and by the greatest possible care to introduce the greatest possible order in political society through its administration.

The claim of the individual to determine his rights for

himself, to do justice in matters pertaining to himself, has
been utterly rejected as inconsistent with order in society; and
in every community, large or small, populous or sparsely
settled, the community determines by an agency of its own
what is right or wrong in the particular case, allowing the
disputant to be heard, but not permitting him to take part in
the decision. Can we suppose that justice is any less the bond
between states, made up of men bound together by justice,
and that the administration of justice between states, which
is the determination of what is just, can be any the less the
principle of order in this larger political society which we
call the society of nations? If we are of this opinion, and
it is hard to see how we can fail to share it, we must seek
to endow the society of nations with that organ or those or-
gans for the determination and the administration of justice,
whether the dispute be between the United States and Japan,
Great Britain and France, Austria-Hungary and Serbia. We
know only too well that the failure to administer justice, re-
sulting in the failure to determine what is just, is and has been
the cause of disorder in political society; and, if it be maintained that there has not been justice between states or enough
conscious justice to determine whether or not it be the
bond between states as between men, and that it is the principle of order between states as between men within one political
society, we certainly have had experience enough to know that
the absence of justice between states and within the society of
nations is the cause of disorder. Would we not better appeal
from Philip drunk to Philip sober, or, more elegantly but
hardly less forcibly expressed, should we not turn our backs
upon these self-constituted sufficiencies the hereditary mon-
archs, and appeal to Aristotle, who still rules in his own right,
not only in one country, but in every country, and not only in
one time, but in all time.

My purpose is not at present to advocate an international
court of justice, but to show that such a court is inevitable
if a society of nations is to exist and if justice is to be

administered; because courts determine what is just in the concrete case and in so doing maintain order in political society, and, because we can not have a law of nations unless there is some agency or means or method created by the society of nations to determine what is just in a particular case, and in such a way as to bind all the members of the society by its decision. There must be some power in international society to determine this for itself, just as the smaller political community determines it, without leaving it to the nations in dispute, any more than a decision is left to the individuals in controversy. The society of nations must become conscious of its existence and of its duties. It must have its representative body to develop the law needed to maintain order among its members, and it must have an agency to interpret and to apply this law in appropriate cases.

The Three Difficulties Which Are Said to Stand in the Way of Creating a Court for the Society of Nations

A great and distinguished friend of mine says that there are three "lions" in the way of the establishment of an international court of justice. The first is the absence of law which the court is to administer; the second is the difficulty of getting the nations before the court, and the third is the difficulty of securing compliance with the judgment when it has been rendered. There are other difficulties, such as a proper and acceptable method of appointing the judges of an international tribunal; but, if the society of nations is conscious of its existence, and if its existence is recognized by each of the members forming it, and, if the solidarity of the civilized nations be a fact, as recognized by the First and Second Hague Peace Conferences, the difficulties in the way of the court may be overcome. The one great obstacle, in my opinion, is the apparent lack of desire on the part of the nations for such a court as shall be the organ of the society and by its decisions bind every member. If the nations really wish such a court, it can easily be created, and the best way to generate a will or a desire is in my opinion not to denounce the nations, as is so frequently done, but to show the existence of the society of nations; to make clear the need of a law of this society and the necessity of a court to ascertain this law and to administer it. Indeed, in my opinion, there is but one difficulty and that is the failure on the part of the nations to appreciate to the full the existence of the society of nations; because if a society exists, and the states admit that it does, it is inevitable that this society should have law and that it should have an organ for its administration.

But let me take up these three difficulties in the way of the court. The first is said to be the absence of law. Now, of course, this is a weighty and a serious reason, because a court administers law, and if law does not exist it must make the law that it is to administer. It is, however, the function of a legislature, not of a court, to make law, although the latter may and does develop the law by its decisions. But do we lack law or do we lack it to the extent suggested in the objection? I believe not. The law of nations is no doubt an imperfect and an inadequate system, but it exists. It may be made more perfect and it may be made adequate to the needs of nations, if it be the desire of the nations so to do, or rather if the nations are convinced that order in political societies depends, as Aristotle asserts, upon the administration of justice. If I am right in supposing that half a dozen principles of municipal law can be considered as the foundation of law, international as well as national; that these principles may be translated into terms of international law and extended as it were beyond the frontiers of the nations into the international domain, the society of nations would have a law as clear and as capable of development as the law of any one of the states belonging to the society of nations. It was to meet and to overcome this first great objection that I have laid such stress upon the necessity of a law for the society of nations, and as a contribution to this subject I shall, as I have already said, submit to the Institute at a subsequent meeting, the bases of the law of nations. But, supposing that the law does not exist, are we to allow ourselves to be discouraged because of this? Are we not, rather, to take steps to bring it into existence? As a partial answer to the contention that the law to be administered by an international court does not exist, I would call your attention to the fact that, although the United States has never codified international law or issued a system of international law as such, there have been decided by the Supreme Court of the United States some 2,800 cases turning upon a principle of international law or in which international law has been involved. This court, which is really international, as it is the agent of forty-eight states claiming to be sovereign, independent and equal in the matter of justice between and among themselves, has apparently not been impressed by the objection that the law did not exist which it was to apply and has seemingly had no great difficulty in ascertaining its principles. Indeed, the fundamental principles of international law which I have laid before you are based upon the fundamental principles of municipal law, and have been stated by the Supreme Court of the United States in judgments which are the best evidence of the existence of international law and of its claim to be considered a branch of jurisprudence. But, leaving out of consideration the judicial decisions of national courts, which, however, exist in every country and deal with questions of international law, an organ already exists which can make and develop the law for the society of nations, according to the desire of the nations themselves. I refer to the Hague Peace Conferences and, without dwelling upon their importance in this place, as I have previously mentioned it, I deem it only necessary to say that even a cursory examination of their work shows that they are none the less law-making, although they may only modestly claim to be law-recommending bodies.

It thus appears that the nations can frame law to be administered by the court, if the law be a prerequisite to the creation of the court, supposing, of course, that the nations are really convinced of the advisability of its establishment and agree to take the steps necessary to call it into being.

The next lion in the way is to get the nations to submit their disputes to the court. The way to do this is by an agreement in the form of a treaty or convention, but this is only the formal not the real difficulty, because there is a widespread fear that the nations may not live up to their agreement to submit disputes. The question thus arises, how can nations that have agreed to resort to the court be compelled to do so? Back of that are the questions whether you can compel nations to live up to their agreements, or whether nations will agree to a treaty or convention allowing force to be used against them in order to compel the submission of disputes of the very kind which they have pledged themselves to lay before the court. Many people whose judgment I respect believe it possible to negotiate an agreement permitting the parties to it to use their forces, as William Penn would say, "united as one strength," to compel the submission of disputes in accordance with the treaty or convention, and indeed to secure by the same means, if necessary, the execution of the judgments of the court if they are not complied with. Personally, I can not bring myself to this point of view, for, however much we may question it, we must rely in the end upon the good faith of nations and, I believe, it is only public opinion which can quicken that faith into action.

The Good Faith of Nations Is Sufficient to Carry Out Their Agreements Under the Pressure of an Enlightened Public Opinion.

Without going into details, I would say that if the nations should agree to submit their justiciable disputes to the court of the society of nations and if, doubting compliance with the pledged word, nations should either conclude a separate agreement or insert in the original treaty or convention a provision for uniting their forces to compel recalcitrant members to lay the dispute of a justiciable nature before the court in accordance with the agreement, we must perforce rely upon the good faith of the nations to live up to their agreement to use force against the recalcitrants. And, even if some few nations should guarantee the execution of the agreement, pledging themselves to combine their forces and either to compel the recalcitrants to submit the case, or to compel the nations parties to the agreement to unite their forces against the recalcitrants, we should have to rely upon the good faith of the few nations to use their forces for this purpose. If we must therefore in the last resort rely upon the good faith of the nations, it seems to me that we should rely upon it in the beginning and not tend to render it ineffective by appearing to doubt it. The same observations apply equally to an agreement to secure by force, if necessary, the execution of a judgment. Therefore, as we must, whether we will or not, rely upon the good faith of nations, it is surely incumbent upon us to refrain from questioning it, and to use every means at our disposal to strengthen a belief in good faith and by so doing to strengthen good faith itself.

The Supreme Court of the United States Is in Form and Procedure the Prototype of the Court for the Society of Nations.

If public opinion is, as I believe, the only force which can be counted upon to compel nations to carry out their promises, we must endeavor to educate public opinion in every country so that the resultant international opinion will be enlightened as well as irresistible. But, fortunately, we do not need to labor this question. The Supreme Court of the United States, which many advocates of an international court of justice regard as the prototype of such an institution, has had an experience of a hundred years and more in settling disputes between states, which, for the purpose of justice, consider themselves as sovereign, independent and equal, and in the course of the century and more of its existence, the Supreme Court has devised a method of procedure which, satisfying the forty-eight sovereign, independent and equal states of the American judicial Union, may at least serve as a basis of procedure likely to be acceptable to the forty-odd states composing the society of nations. As I intend to lay a project of an international judiciary before the Institute at a later meeting, it is perhaps unwise to enter into details at this time. I would like to call your attention to the fact that the Constitution of the United States, which creates what may be called, for present purposes, a judicial union, provides that state may sue state in the Supreme Court of the United States. And I would like to lay before you some observations of a general kind upon the practice of the Supreme Court considered in fact if not in theory as an international tribunal.

It is inherent in the nature of a court to determine its competence, and, as the states have agreed to sue one another in questions concerning law and equity, it is necessary for the court before taking jurisdiction to satisfy itself that the suit is between states and that it involves a principle of law or of equity. In other words, the court determines whether the parties have a right to appear before the court, that is to say, whether it has jurisdiction of the parties and whether it has jurisdiction of the case; whether the dispute is justiciable, whether it involves law or equity.

A doubt having arisen as to the right of the mixed commission, organized under Article VII of the Jay Treaty of 1794 between Great Britain and the United States, to determine its jurisdiction, the matter was referred to Lord Loughborough, then Lord Chancellor of England, who replied "that the doubt respecting the authority of the commissioners to settle their own jurisdiction was absurd; and that they must necessarily decide upon cases being within, or without, their competency."[1]

In a very carefully considered and long-drawn-out boundary dispute between Rhode Island and Massachusetts, two states of the American judicial union, the Supreme Court considered at length and in great detail the nature of a justiciable ques-

---

[1] Moore's International Arbitrations, Vol. I, p. 327.

tion, and the difference between it and a political one.[1] From
time to time the Court has found itself obliged to reconsider
this question, which it has likewise treated as a julicial one.
It may therefore be said that as far as the United States is concerned the distinction between a justiciable question and a
political one has been clearly determined in judicial proceedings. There seems to be no valid reason why an international
court composed of judges as eminent as those who have
adorned the Supreme bench of the United States could not
be trusted to determine what is or is not a justiciable question,
and to refuse, as does the Supreme Court of the United States,
to take jurisdiction in political questions.

But to return to the "lion" which bars the way. How is a
state which has agreed to submit its justiciable questions to
a court to be compelled to live up to its agreement? The experience of the Supreme Court in this matter is enlightening.
In the case of *New Jersey* v. *New York*,[2] decided in 1830,
the Supreme Court stated that it would, upon the request of
the plaintiff state, direct that a subpoena be issued out of the
Court against the state of New York and served upon the
Governor and Attorney General of the state, commanding
them to appear within the space of sixty days. The subpoena
was issued. It was served upon the Governor and the Attorney General of the state, and yet the state did not make
its appearance by its appropriate agent. In these circumstances, the Court decided that the state of New Jersey could
proceed *ex parte* in the absence of the defendant and that a
judgment would be entered against the state of New York
by default.[3] Also the Court held in the case of *Massachusetts* v. *Rhode Island* that if a defendant state had appeared,
it might withdraw its appearance. Indeed, it further stated
that "no coercive measure will be taken to compel appearance."[4] As the result of these proceedings we have it laid

---

[1] 2 Peters' Reports, 657.
[2] 3 Peters' Reports, 461.
[3] 5 Peters' Reports, 284.
[4] 12 Peters' Reports, 755.

down that a state may sue another state of the American Union; that the defendant will be summoned, if the suit between the two states is of a justiciable nature; that the appearance of the defendant is left to its good faith acting under the spur of public opinion, for the Court expressly declares that coercive measures to compel the appearance of the state will not be used.

In like manner, the Supreme Court has held that there is no power on the part of the United States to compel by force the execution of any judgment of the Supreme Court against a state, saying, in the leading case of *Kentucky* v. *Dennison:* "If the Governor of Ohio refuses to discharge this duty [of surrendering a fugitive from justice in accordance with the provision of the Constitution and a law of Congress] there is no power delegated to the general Government, either through the Judicial Department or any other department, to use any coercive means to compel him."[1]

It may also be mentioned in this connection that the Supreme Court modifies in suits between states the procedure that would otherwise be employed in suits between individuals in such a way as to permit the defendant state to present its defense, while safeguarding the right of the plaintiff state to lay its full case before the Court, so that the dispute may be considered and be decided upon its merits.[2] From these simple statements, does it not appear that we have here a prototype of an international court and of its procedure? The nations can form a judicial union, just as they have formed many public unions, notably the Postal Union, to which not only all independent states but self-governing colonies are parties. They may agree that their disputes of a justiciable nature shall be submitted to and decided by the court of the judicial union, which, like its American prototype, will determine before taking jurisdiction that the case is one between state and state parties to the union; that the dispute, as presented is justiciable; that the defendant state is to be invited to appear, not to be

[1] 24 Howard's Reports, 66, 109–10.
[2] Rhode Island v. Massachusetts, 14 Peters' Reports, 210.

compelled by force to litigate the dispute; that, in the absence of the defendant state, the plaintiff state may present its case and if it be supported by evidence and be justified in law a judgment will be rendered, even in the absence of the defendant, but that compliance with the judgment, like the appearance of the defendant, depends upon the good faith of the states. There is no superior in the society of nations and an agreement creating an international court of justice for the decision of their justiciable disputes simply creates an agency for the purposes of justice, but does not make of the court a superior, with power to compel appearance and with power to enforce obedience to its judgments. The experience of the Supreme Court shows that good faith alone, acting under the pressure of public opinion is sufficient. Is not the good faith of nations to be trusted, as we trust the good faith of the states of the American Union, and is not the public opinion of the society of nations likely to be as powerful, if not more powerful than the public opinion of one of them?

The Court of the Society of Nations Must, as in the American System, Determine the Lawfulness of the Acts of the Society and of Its Members.

Before concluding, for I am painfully conscious that I have taxed your patience well nigh to the breaking point, let me refer again to the function of a court of law, which seems so elemental to us of the northern republic that we are in danger of overlooking it or of not attaching to it sufficient importance.

I have frequently said, indeed I have constantly, consciously and repeatedly said, that the American conception of the state is that of a body politic created by the people for their safety and happiness, with a form of government calculated to secure to the people the enjoyment of their inalienable rights, among which are life, liberty, and the pursuit of happiness. The conception of the state as a body politic carries with it as a corollary that the body politic is a creature of the people and organized by them for certain specific purposes, as is and must be a corporation; that the state as such can neither have nor exercise rights which are not granted or allowed to it by the people, and that the government created by the people is invested with certain rights and with certain duties in order to fulfil the purpose for which it, as well as the state was created, namely, to contribute to the safety and happiness of the people. This means to an American that the state itself is subordinated to law because it can only do that which it has been authorized by law to do; that the government is likewise subordinated to law; and that all the acts of both are tested by law. If they are found to be within the grant of power, the acts are valid. If they are found to be in excess of the grant, they are invalid.

The government does not and the officers of the government interested in the exercise of power do not pass upon these questions. In the American system, the judiciary sits in judgment upon the acts of the highest officers, letting them stand if there is a warrant for them in law, quashing them if they are contrary to law. In the American system the legislature is a body invested with certain rights and denied others. If an act thereof is within the grant of power, it is valid; if it be in excess of the grant, it is invalid. But, as in the case of the government, neither the legislature nor the members thereof pass upon the validity of their acts; the court of justice determines whether the act is or is not in accordance with the grant. Finally, in the American system, the rights and duties of the Executive Department, the rights and duties of the Legislative Department, and the functions of the Judiciary are stated and defined in the constitution, which reserves to the people the rights which have not been specifically granted away.

Law has always been looked upon in the English-speaking colonies as the bulwark of their rights and of their liberties. The colonists had to know exactly the nature and extent of their charters in order that they might not be deprived of their rights. In the contest between the body politic or corporation called the colony or province, and the larger corporation known as England, the necessity of understanding the sphere rightfully claimed and exercised by each, made knowledge of the law essential. An act of the colony in excess of its grant was set aside. It was natural, therefore, that the new states, familiar with this process, should invest their courts with the faculty of testing the rightful exercise of power by the United States, by any department of the government, or by the state as against the government, or by the legislature within the state. The United States was the first country in the world to have the acts of the government and of the congress passed upon by the courts, to be set aside if inconsistent with the constitutional grant of power. The American system is indeed a government of laws, not of men, and the distinguished American publicist, the Honorable Simeon E. Baldwin, whose authority I have invoked on a previous occasion, finely summed up the effect of the separation of the colonies from Great Britain when he said: "Loyalty to law took the place of loyalty to king."

The acceptance of the American conception of the state requires the acceptance of the American doctrine that the acts of the state, irrespective of the official character of the person who has commited the acts, shall be subordinate, not superior, to the constitution, and that the validity of these acts shall be tested by a court of justice applying the fundamental law of the constitution to the act called in question. For, as the distinguished diplomat, jurist and statesman, the late Edward J. Phelps, has truly and happily said:

> American experience has made it an axiom in political science that no written constitution of government can hope to stand without a paramount and independent tribunal to determine its construction and to enforce its precepts in the last resort. This is the great and foremost duty cast by the Constitution, for the sake of the Constitution, upon the Supreme Court of the United States.[1]

[1]Orations and Essays of Edward John Phelps, 1901, pp. 58–59.

Coöperation not Federation of Nations Is the World's Need

Are we to rest content with the loose and ill-defined union which we call the society of nations, or are we to create by conscious effort a federated state? Instead of perfecting what we have, are we to create something differing in kind as well as in degree? Many people advocate a world state, that is, they look upon the states of the world as merged into a federal state or as forming parts of a universal state. But it seems to me doubtful whether such a state be possible and if possible whether it is desirable. In any event, its creation seems to be so remote, depending as it does upon the conscious renunciation of independence, although equality is maintained, that we may be pardoned if we content ourselves at least for the present with more modest proposals.

We can not hope to realize our ambitions at a bound. Progress is not by revolution, but through a continuous, successive series of small changes. From earliest childhood we are familiar with this truth, but it is to be feared that when we grow up we do indeed put away childish things and forget the lines, as applicable to the world at large as they are to the nursery, concerning "little drops of water and little grains of sand." We must be content to make haste slowly, if the work of our hands is to stand the test of our successors and if it is to be in itself a round in the ladder of progress. We should, I think, insist upon coöperation or common action toward a common end, the end being the common good of nations. We must frankly recognize the existence of the society of nations, composed of nations equal and independent; that these nations are united as the Hague Conferences have said by solidarity, and that every action taken be measured in terms of the general interest.

The question arises, how can these nations best coöperate? Put in this form, the question answers itself, for they can not in a common interest very well work apart. I think and I have long thought that we should consciously try to do on a large scale what has been done well and successfully on a small scale, in the hope that each step forward will be an incentive to a further step, and that little by little the problem will solve itself. We should not relax our efforts if what we accomplish does not seem to advance the cause or fit appreciably into the general scheme of things. Logic has its place in the schools, but history is not necessarily logical. Political science is a thing of practice and of experience. The test is not whether a thing is logically perfect, but whether it works well, whether it accomplishes the purpose for which it was created. When sufficient progress has been made, we can then see whither we are tending and perhaps discover a general principle by the aid of which we may accelerate the rate of progress. Very often the little things lay down the great principle. Very often private initiative points the way to official action. This slow, tentative, hesitating, experimental method is, I think, more necessary in international than in national relations, because nations are fearful, and properly so, lest they take a false step. If an individual makes a mistake, he may undo its consequences, but a nation may by a false step jeopardize its existence, or by entering into an untried agreement it may sacrifice or seem to sacrifice its independence.

The Universal Postal Union Is the Type of a Coöperative Union

In the past fifty or sixty years we have had experience with the so-called international unions, some of which are of a private, others of a public, nature. Each union deals with a specific subject, and the possibility of the union has been tested by results. The nations taking part in the creation of the union did so because they felt that the union might do good and, as they were free to withdraw, they felt they could safely be parties to its creation and in its operation. Take as an example the Universal Postal Union, to which all independent nations and to which also self-governing colonies are signatories. This union was formed in 1874, upon the initiative of Germany, and the revised convention today in force was signed at Rome on May 26, 1906. The fact that self-governing colonies or dominions are members means and can only mean that sovereignty is not involved, because if it were, self-governing but not sovereign communities conld not be members.

The fact is, something needed to be done and each state and self-governing community had an interest in having it done. It was natural that what concerned all should be done by all, that the nations should come together, that they should coöperate, that they should take common action for a common purpose toward a common goal, namely, the transmission of postal correspondence to, from and through each of them.

They felt that differences of opinion might arise and they appreciated the advantage of settling these differences by peaceful means. They therefore provided in Article 43 that any differences of opinion or disputes arising between postal administrations, or that any differences of opinion as to the interpretation of the convention should be submitted to arbitration, each disputant appointing an arbiter and the two selecting an umpire. It was evident to the partisans of this union that the nations should meet regularly at stated times to revise the convention, and this has been done. It was foreseen that the successful operation of the union would require administrative machinery. Therefore, a permanent office of the union was created at Berne. All this seems simple enough. It has come about so naturally and so quietly that we hardly take note of its existence; yet this Universal Postal Convention not only points the way, but is the way to international organization, because it creates a union of the nations having a common interest in postal matters.

It provides for a periodic meeting of representatives of the contracting powers to legislate in postal matters. From this standpoint, it may be called a legislative union, although restricted to matters of postal correspondence.

It also provides a method of settling differences of opinion and disputes between and among its members and for the authoritative interpretation of the convention. In this aspect, it is a judicial union.

It further provides for a central office to look after the interests of the union, and to see that its provisions are carried out. In this respect it is an administrative union in postal matters.

I could illustrate the same process of development by citing other public unions, likewise of a special kind, but the Postal Union is sufficient for present purposes. May we not properly ask whether the time will not come, if it is not already at hand, to consolidate these different unions, with the result that we shall have for many purposes a legislative union, a judicial union and an administrative union from those which already exist?

My purpose, however, is not at present to enter further into details, but to show how easy it would be for the nations to tread, as it were, in their own footsteps and to organize a union differing in degree rather than in kind from those which already exist. It is pertinent, however, to ask ourselves, is it necessary to organize a union? Does not the union which we have in mind already exist, although we do not seem to be conscious, as we ought to be, of its existence? The society of nations is a union, however loose and indefinite it may be when compared with the conscious, definite, restricted postal union. The Hague Conference, meeting at stated periods, would be a legislature, not in the national but in the international sense, which is another way of saying that it is a diplomatic body which does not enact laws, but which recommends treaties and conventions for the ratification of the nations taking part in its proceedings. If it has been found possible for the nations to agree to settle by arbitration disputes arising under the postal convention, including its interpretation or application, can not these same nations agree to constitute in advance of the dispute an arbitral or a judicial body for the trial and disposition of disputes when and as they arise? When this is done, the society of nations will have a judicial union. The first step towards it, and that a very long one, was taken in 1899 at the First Hague Conference, by the creation of the so-called Permanent Court of Arbitration. The administrative council at The Hague, composed as it is of the nations accredited to the Netherlands, could act either as a body or through committees as the administrative organ of the society.

Suarez on the Society and Law of Nations

A great and a learned Spaniard, one Suarez by name, thus stated in classic terms in the early days of the seventeenth century the need of a society of nations and of a law to regulate the conduct of its members:

> The human race, however divided into various peoples and kingdoms, has always not only its unity as a species but also a certain moral and quasi-political unity, pointed out by the natural precept of mutual love and pity which extends to all, even to foreigners of any nation. Wherefore although every perfect state, whether a republic or a kingdom, is in itself a perfect community composed of its own members, still each such state, viewed in relation to the human race, is in some measure a member of that universal unity. For those communities are never singly so self-sufficing but that they stand in need of some mutual aid, society and communion, sometimes for the improvement of their condition and their greater commodity, but sometimes also for their moral necessity and need, as appears by experience. For that reason they are in need of some law by which they may be directed and rightly ordered in that kind of communion and society. And although this is to a great extent supplied by natural reason, yet it is not so supplied sufficiently and immediately for all purposes, and therefore it has been possible for particular laws to be introduced by the practice (*usu*) of those same nations. For just as custom (*consuetudo*) introduces law in a state or province, so it was possible for laws to be introduced in the whole human race by the habitual conduct (*moribus*) of nations. And that all the more because the points which belong to this law are few and approach very nearly to natural law, and

being easily deduced from it are useful and agreeable to nature, so that although this law can not be plainly deduced as being altogether necessary in itself to laudable conduct (*ad honestatem morum*), still it is very suitable to nature and such as all may accept for its own sake.[1]

We look upon recent events, such as the Hague Conferences, as establishing this union, whereas in fact it existed, and must have existed, from the very moment that intercourse of independent states was permitted, because recognized as a necessity. The First Hague Conference of 1899 brought this simple truth home to the most bourgeois among us, and indeed our state of mind at the present day is largely comparable to that of Monsieur Jourdain, when he learned that he had been writing prose:

Monsieur Jourdain. Now let me tell you something in confidence. I am in love with a lady of high rank and I want you to help me to write her a little note which I intend to drop at her feet.
Professor of Philosophy. Certainly.
Monsieur Jourdain. That would be a gallant thing to do; wouldn't it?
Professor of Philosophy. Undoubtedly. Do you want to write it in verse?
Monsieur Jourdain. No, no, not verse.
Professor of Philosophy. You prefer mere prose?
Monsieur Jourdain. No, I don't want either prose or verse.
Professor of Philosophy. But you must have one or the other.
Monsieur Jourdain. Why?
Professor of Philosophy. Because, monsieur, there is no way to express ourselves except in prose or verse.
Monsieur Jourdain. Is there nothing but prose and verse?
Professor of Philosophy. Nothing, monsieur. All that is not prose is verse; all that is not verse is prose.
Monsieur Jourdain. When we talk, what's that?
Professor of Philosophy. Prose.

[1]Tractatus de Legibus et Deo Legislatore, 2, 19, 9 (1611); translated in The Collected Papers of John Westlake on Public International Law, 1914, p. 27.

Monsieur Jourdain. What! when I say, "Nicole, bring me my slippers and give me my night-cap," is that prose?
Professor of Philosophy. Yes, monsieur.
Monsieur Jourdain. Good Heavens! I've been talking prose these forty years and never knew it. I am certainly very much obliged to you for teaching me that.[1]

I have dwelt at considerable length upon these matters, because the burning question at the present day is the organization of the society of nations in such a way as to secure the administration of justice between the states which will assuredly prove to be the principle of order in this larger political society as it has proved itself to be such in the smaller political society with which we are more familiar. I have tried to show that the society of nations exists; that if it exists it must have a law; that if it has a law it must have some authoritative agent to interpret this law and to apply it to the disputes which must needs arise between the members of the society.

That the American Institute, composed of an equal number of representative publicists from each national society created in every one of the twenty-one American republics shall bring to bear upon the world the fact that a society of nations exists; that there is a solidarity among its members; that a law is needed to regulate the conduct of each nation toward all others within the society, and that there must be an agency to develop and to create this law, as well as an agency to ascertain it and to apply it to the disputes whenever they shall arise between nations, is the hope not only of its founders, of the national societies with which it will coöperate, of all right-minded men, but also of all men of good will, for the peace which is the perfected fruit of justice is the promise of the Gospel only to men of good will.

---

[1]Molière: Le Bourgeois Gentilhomme, Act II, Scene iv.

REMARKS ON INTRODUCING THE DECLARATION OF THE RIGHTS AND DUTIES OF NATIONS, JANUARY 6, 1916.

GENTLEMEN:

It is my very great pleasure, in pursuance of a promise made in a previous session, to lay before you a project which, if it should meet with your approval, will, I venture to hope, supply a firm and secure foundation upon which the temple of American justice can safely rest. It is a very ambitious project, and I therefore submit it to your consideration with no little misgiving.

At a time when the very existence of international law is being questioned, it is incumbent upon us to examine with great care the fundamental principles upon which the law of nations must rest if there either is or is to be a system of justice between nations, to ascertain and to state those principles, and to bring them home to every man of light and leading in the continent. It is our duty as well as our privilege to devise a method not merely for the dissemination of a knowledge and an understanding of them but a method of developing them in such a way that rules, based upon these fundamental principles, shall be formulated in order that there may be a standard of conduct common to the American Republics, based upon a system of justice not only common to them but deeply imbedded in the life and thought of their citizens, in the full consciousness that the principles of justice and the rules of conduct acceptable to the American Republics are capable of a universal application.

It has seemed to me that no great good would come from a discussion of the rules of conduct in isolated cases and that, even with the greatest good will in the world and although armed with industry and devotion, we could do little in this way and in this first session calculated to improve or to advance the law of nations. The different projects which have been proposed for study and investigation are indeed admirable, but to make progress upon an uncharted sea we must be sure of the point of departure and the goal which we would reach. Let me reënforce these views by the language of a great American statesman, particularly applicable to the storm and stress in which we exist rather than live, and let me express the hope that his words of wisdom may be as a glass to the eye and as a lamp to our feet. In the very first words of his reply to Hayne, Daniel Webster said:

> When the mariner has been tossed for many days in thick weather, and on an unknown sea, he naturally avails himself of the first pause in the storm, the earliest glance of the sun, to take his latitude, and ascertain how far the elements have driven him from his true course. Let us imitate this prudence, and before we float farther on the waves of this debate, refer to the point from which we departed, that we may at least be able to conjecture where we now are.[1]

In justification of the large part which duty plays in the project which I am about to lay before you, let me quote the language of another great statesman of my country, whose reputation is not confined to the United States and whose name is as a household word in the American Republics. On opening the Conference of Teachers of International Law in the City of Washington in 1914, Mr. Elihu Root said:

> I think no one can study the movement of the times without realizing the democracy of the world—for it is not alone in this country—is realizing its rights in advance of a realization of its duties. And that way lies disaster, that way lies hideous wrong, that way lies the exercise of the mighty powers of modern democracies to destroy themselves, to destroy the vitality of the princi-

---

[1] Whipple's "Great Speeches and Orations of Daniel Webster," 1879, p. 227.

ples upon which they depend. . . . Unless the popular will responds to the instructed and competent leadership of opinion upon the vital question of our foreign relations, the worst impulses of democracy will control. At the bottom of wise and just action lies an understanding of national rights and national duties. Half the wars of history have come because of mistaken opinions as to national rights and national obligations, have come from the unthinking assumption that all the right is on the side of one's own country, all the duty on the side of some other country.[1]

Gentlemen, I ask your consideration of a proposed Declaration of the Rights and Duties of Nations, preceded by a preamble and followed by a commentary.

---

[1]Root's Addresses on International Subjects, 1916, pp. 127-8.

DECLARATION OF THE RIGHTS AND DUTIES OF NATIONS
adopted by the American Institute of International Law at its first session in the City of Washington, January 6, 1916

WHEREAS the municipal law of civilized nations recognizes and protects the right to life, the right to liberty, the right to the pursuit of happiness, as added by the Declaration of Independence of the United States of America, the right to legal equality, the right to property, and the right to the enjoyment of the aforesaid rights; and

WHEREAS these fundamental rights, thus universally recognized, create a duty on the part of the peoples of all nations to observe them; and

WHEREAS, according to the political philosophy of the Declaration of Independence of the United States, and the universal practice of the American Republics, nations or governments are regarded as created by the people, deriving their just powers from the consent of the governed, and are instituted among men to promote their safety and happiness and to secure to the people the enjoyment of their fundamental rights; and

WHEREAS the nation is a moral or juristic person, the creature of law, and subordinated to law as is the natural person in political society; and

WHEREAS we deem that these fundamental rights can be stated in terms of international law and applied to the relations of the members of the society of nations, one with another, just as they have been applied in the relations of the citizens or subjects of the states forming the Society of Nations; and

WHEREAS these fundamental rights of national jurisprudence, namely, the right to life, the right to liberty, the right to the pursuit of happiness, the right to equality before the law, the right to property, and the right to the observance thereof are, when stated in terms of international law, the right of the nation to exist and to protect and to conserve its existence; the right of independence and the freedom to develop itself without interference or control from other nations; the right of equality in law and before law; the right to territory within defined boundaries and to exclusive jurisdiction therein; and the right to the observance of these fundamental rights; and

WHEREAS the rights and the duties of nations are, by virtue of membership in the society thereof, to be exercised and performed in accordance with the exigencies of their mutual Interdependence expressed in the preamble to the Convention for the Pacific Settlement of International Disputes of the First and Second Hague Peace Conferences, recognizing the solidarity which unites the members of the society of civilized nations;

THEREFORE, THE AMERICAN INSTITUTE OF INTERNATIONAL LAW, at its first session, held in the City of Washington, in the United States of America, on the sixth day of January, 1916, adopts the following six articles, together with the commentary thereon, to be known as its

Declaration of the Rights and Duties of Nations

I. Every nation has the right to exist, and to protect and to conserve its existence; but this right neither implies the right nor justifies the act of the state to protect itself or to conserve its existence by the commission of unlawful acts against innocent and unoffending states.

II. Every nation has the right to independence in the sense that, it has a right to the pursuit of happiness and is free to develop itself without interference or control from other states, provided that in so doing it does not interfere with or violate the rights of other states.

III. Every nation is in law and before law the equal of every other nation belonging to the society of nations, and all nations have the right to claim and, according to the Declaration of Independence of the United States, "to assume, among the powers of the earth, the separate and equal station to which the laws of nature and of nature's God entitle them."

IV. Every nation has the right to territory within defined boundaries and to exercise exclusive jurisdiction over its territory, and all persons whether native or foreign found therein.

V. Every nation entitled to a right by the law of nations is entitled to have that right respected and protected by all other nations, for right and duty are correlative, and the right of one is the duty of all to observe.

VI. International law is at one and the same time both national and international: national in the sense that it is the law of the land and applicable as such to the decision of all questions involving its principles; international in the sense that it is the law of the society of nations and applicable as such to all questions between and among the members of the society of nations involving its principles.

Official Commentary upon the Declaration of the Rights and Duties of Nations, adopted January 6, 1916.

I. Every nation has the right to exist, and to protect and to conserve its existence; but this right neither implies the right nor justifies the act of the state to protect itself or to conserve its existence by the commission of unlawful acts against innocent and unoffending states.

This right is to be understood in the sense in which the right to life is understood in national law, according to which it is unlawful for a human being to take human life, unless it be necessary so to do in self-defense against an unlawful attack threatening the life of the party unlawfully attacked.

In the Chinese Exclusion Case (reported in 130 United States Reports, pp. 581, 606), decided by the Supreme Court of the United States in 1888, Mr. Justice Field said for the Court:

> To preserve its independence, and give security against foreign aggression and encroachment, is the highest duty of every nation, and to attain these ends nearly all other considerations are to be subordinated. It matters not in what form such aggression and encroachment come, whether from the foreign nation acting in its national character or from vast hordes of its people crowding in upon us. The government, possessing the powers which are to be exercised for protection and security, is clothed with authority to determine the occasion on which the powers shall be called forth; and its determination, so far as the subjects affected are concerned, are necessarily conclusive upon all its departments and officers.

The right of a state to exist and to protect and to conserve its existence is to be understood in the sense in which the right of an individual to his life was defined, interpreted and applied in terms applicable alike to nations and individuals in the well known English case of *Regina vs. Dudley* (reported in 15 Cox's Criminal Cases, p. 624; 14 Queen's Bench Division, p. 273), decided by the Queen's Bench Division of the High Court of Justice in 1884, to the effect that it was unlawful for shipwrecked sailors to take the life of one of their number, in order to preserve their own lives, because it was unlawful according to the common law of England for an English subject to take human life, unless to defend himself against an unlawful attack of the assailant threatening the life of the party unlawfully attacked.

The right of a State to exist and to protect and to conserve its existence, as laid down by the Supreme Court of the United States, is recognized not merely in the United States but in Latin America, as appears from the views of the well-known publicists, Messrs. Bello and Calvo, who may be considered representative of Latin American thought and practice.

Thus Bello, writing in 1832, said:

> There is no doubt that every nation has the right of self-preservation and is entitled to take protective measures against any danger whatsoever; but this danger must be great, manifest and imminent, in order to make it lawful for us to exact by force that another nation alter its institutions for our benefit. (Andrés Bello, *Principios de Derecho de Jentes*, part 1, chap. 1, VII.)

And Calvo, half a century later, said:

> One of the essential rights inherent in the sovereignty and the independence of States is that of self-preservation. This right is the first of all absolute or permanent rights and is the fundamental basis of a great number of accessory, secondary, or occasional rights. We may say that it constitutes the supreme law of nations, as well as the most imperative duty of citizens, and a society that fails to repel aggression from without neglects its moral duties toward its members and fails to live up to the very purpose of its institution. (Carlos Calvo, *Le Droit International Théorique et Pratique*, 5th ed., Vol. 1, § 208.)

II. Every nation has the right to independence in the sense that, it has a right to the pursuit of happiness and is free to develop itself without interference or control from other states, provided that in so doing it does not interfere with or violate the rights of other states.

III. Every nation is in law and before law the equal of every other state composing the society of nations, and all nations have the right to claim and, according to the Declaration of Independence of the United States, "to assume, among the powers of the earth, the separate and equal station to which the laws of nature and of nature's God entitle them."

The right to independence and its necessary corollary, equality, is to be understood in the sense in which it was defined in the following passage quoted from the decision of the great English admiralty judge, Sir William Scott, later Lord Stowell, in the case of *The Louis* (reported in 2 Dodson's Reports, pp. 210, 243-44), decided in 1817:

> Two principles of public law are generally recognized as fundamental. One is the perfect equality and entire independence of all distinct states. Relative magnitude creates no distinction of right; relative imbecility, whether permanent or casual, gives no additional right to the more powerful neighbor; and any advantage seized upon that ground is mere usurpation. This is the great foundation of public law, which it mainly concerns the peace of mankind, both in their politic and private capacities, to preserve inviolate. The second is, that all nations being equal, all have an equal right to the uninterrupted use of the unappropriated parts of the ocean for their navigation. In places where no local authority exists, where the subjects of all states meet upon a footing of entire equality and independence, no one state, or any of its subjects, has a right to assume or exercise authority over the subjects of another.

The right of equality is also to be understood in the sense in which it was stated and illustrated by John Marshall, Chief Justice of the Supreme Court of the United States, who said, in deciding the case of *The Antelope,* in 1825 (reported in 10 Wheaton's Reports, pp. 66, 122) :

> In this commerce thus sanctioned by universal assent, every nation had an equal right to engage. How is this right to be lost? Each may renounce it for its own people; but can this renunciation affect others?
>
> No principle of general law is more universally acknowledged, than the perfect equality of nations. Russia and Geneva have equal rights. It results from this equality, that no one can rightfully impose a rule on another. Each legislates for itself, but its legislation can operate on itself alone. A right, then, which is vested in all, by the consent of all, can be divested only by consent; and this [slave] trade, in which all have participated, must remain lawful to those who can not be induced to relinquish it. As no nation can prescribe a rule for others, none can make a law of nations; and this traffic remains lawful to those whose governments have not forbidden it.

The right of equality is further to be understood in the sense in which it was expressed and illustrated by Mr. Elihu Root, in the following passage from the address which he delivered, when Secretary of State of the United States, and in the presence of the official delegates of the American Republics accredited to the Third Pan American Conference held at Rio de Janeiro on July 31, 1906:

> We wish for no victories but those of peace; for no territory except our own; for no sovereignty except the sovereignty over ourselves. We deem the independence and equal rights of the smallest and weakest member of the family of nations entitled to as much respect as those of the greatest empire, and we deem the observance of that respect the chief guaranty of the weak against the oppression of the strong. We neither claim nor desire any rights, or privileges, or powers that we do not freely concede to every American Republic. We wish to increase our prosperity, to expand our trade, to grow in wealth, in wisdom, and in spirit, but our conception of

the true way to accomplish this is not to pull down others and profit by their ruin, but to help all friends to a common prosperity and a common growth, that we may all become greater and stronger together.

It would seem that the measured judgments of Lord Stowell and of Chief Justice Marshall, not to speak of Mr. Root's opinion, given as Secretary of State, are sufficient to establish a principle of international law, and that it is unnecessary to cite other authorities, if the ones already quoted fail to produce conviction. In order to show, however, that independence and equality are the law of the American Continent, the authority of the two great Latin American publicists may be again invoked.

Thus, Bello says:

> From the independence and the sovereignty of nations it follows that no one nation is permitted to dictate to any other nation the form of government, of religion, or of administration that it must adopt, or to hold it accountable for the relations between its citizens or those between the government and its subjects. (Bello, *Principios de Derecho de Jentes,* part 1, chap. 1, VII.)

> All men being equal, the groups of men composing universal society are equal. The weakest republic enjoys the same rights and is subject to the same duties as the mightiest empire. (Bello, *Principios de Derecho de Jentes,* part 1, chap. 1, II.)

And to the same effect, but more at length, Calvo says:

> States possess, by virtue of the law of their organization and of their sovereignty, their own exclusive and particular sphere of action. In this respect, they depend upon no one and are bound to provide for the maintenance of those rights and for the observance of those duties alone which are the fundamental and necessary basis of every free society. Absolute sovereignty necessarily implies complete independence. Hence States, in so far as they are moral persons, have a fundamental right: the right of freely carrying out their destinies; and

a duty that is no less imperative: the duty of recognizing and of respecting the sovereign rights and the absolute independence of other States. (Calvo, *Le Droit International Théorique et Pratique,* 5th ed., Vol. I, § 107.)

The equality of sovereign States is a generally recognized principle of public law. It has the twofold consequence of giving all States the same rights and of imposing upon them the same mutual duties. The relative size of their territories cannot justify, in this regard, the slightest difference or the slightest distinction between nations considered as moral persons, and, from the point of view of international law, as well as from that of equity, what is lawful or unjust for one State is likewise lawful or unjust for all others. "Nothing can be done to a small or weak nation," said Mr. Sumner in the United States Senate on March 23, 1871, "that would not be done to a large or powerful nation, or that we would not allow to be done to ourselves." (Calvo, *Le Droit International Théorique et Pratique,* 5th ed., Vol. I, § 210.)

IV. **Every nation has the right to territory within defined boundaries and to exercise exclusive jurisdiction over its territory, and all persons whether native or foreign found therein.**

This right is to be understood in the sense in which it was stated by Chief Justice Marshall in the following passage of his judgment in the case of the schooner *Exchange* (reported in 7 Cranch's Reports, pp. 116, 136-7), decided by the Supreme Court of the United States in the year 1812:

The jurisdiction of the nation, within its own territory, is necessarily exclusive and absolute; it is susceptible of no limitation, not imposed by itself. Any restriction upon it, deriving validity from an external source, would imply a diminution of its sovereignty, to the extent of the restriction, and an investment of that sovereignty, to the same extent, in that power which could impose such restriction. All exceptions, therefore, to the full and complete power of a nation, within its own territories, must be traced up to the consent of the nation itself. They can flow from no other legitimate source.

This consent may be either express or implied. In the latter case, it is less determinate, exposed more to the uncertainties of construction; but, if understood, not less obligatory. The world being composed of distinct sovereignties, possessing equal rights and equal independence, whose mutual benefit is promoted by intercourse with each other, and by an interchange of those good offices which humanity dictates and its wants require, all sovereignties have consented to a relaxation, in practice, in cases under certain peculiar circumstances, of that absolute and complete jurisdiction within their respective territories which sovereignty confers. This consent may, in some instances, be tested by common usage, and by common opinion, growing out of that usage. A nation would justly be considered as violating its faith, although that faith might not be expressly plighted, which should suddenly and without previous notice, exercise its territorial powers in a manner not consonant to the usages and received obligations of the civilized world. . . .

This perfect equality and absolute independence of sovereigns, and this common interest impelling them to mutual intercourse, and an interchange of good offices with each other, have given rise to a class of cases in which every sovereign is understood to waive the exercise of a part of that complete exclusive territorial jurisdiction, which has been stated to be the attribute of every nation.

In view of the fulness of Chief Justice Marshall's exposition of this right and its consequences, and in view also of the acceptance of *The Exchange* as an authority in every civilized country, both as to the right and its limitation, it does not seem necessary to quote statements of Latin-American publicists, in order to sustain what may be called the obvious, and which is deeply imbedded in the legislation of the American Republics.

In lieu of many illustrations that might be drawn from the civil codes of the Latin-American States, one will suffice, namely, Article 14 of the civil code of Chile, which declares that, the law is binding upon all the inhabitants of the Republic, including foreigners.

V. Every nation entitled to a right by the law of nations is entitled to have that right respected and protected by all other nations, for right and duty are correlative, and the right of one is the duty of all to observe.

This right is to be understood in the sense in which it was stated in the following passage from the judgment of Chief Justice Waite in the case of *United States vs. Arjona* (reported in 120 United States Reports, pp. 479, 487), decided by the Supreme Court of the United States in 1886, holding that as each nation had by international law the exclusive right to fix its standard of money, it was the duty of the United States as a member of the Society of Nations to protect the money of a foreign country, in this case Colombia, from forgery:

> But if the United States can require this of another, that other may require it of them, because international obligations are of necessity reciprocal in their nature. The right, if it exists at all, is given by the law of nations, and what is law for one is, under the same circumstances, law for the other. A right secured by the law of nations to a nation, or its people, is one the United States as the representatives of this nation are bound to protect.

VI. International law is at one and the same time both national and international: national in the sense that it is the law of the land and applicable as such to the decision of all questions involving its principles; international in the sense that it is the law of the society of nations and applicable as such to all questions between and among the members of the society of nations involving its principles.

International law, then called the law of nations, was declared by judges and commentators before the Declaration of Independence of the United States to form an integral part of the common law of England, and by judges and commentators of the United States as adopted at one and the same time with the adoption of the common law of which it formed an integral part. Thus, in the case of *Buvot v. Barbuit* (reported in Cases Tempore Talbot, p. 281), decided by Lord Chancellor Talbot in 1733, that distinguished judge and upright man is reported by Lord Mansfield, who was then the ornament of the bar and was counsel in the case, to have said:

> That the law of nations, in its full extent, was part of the law of England. That the act of Parliament was declaratory, and occasioned by a particular incident. That the law of nations was to be collected from the practice of different nations, and the authority of writers.

In the case of *Triquet v. Bath* (reported in 3 Burrow, p. 1478), decided by the Court of King's Bench in 1764, Lord Chief Justice Mansfield held, quoting the judgment of Lord Talbot in *Buvot v. Barbuit,* that the law of nations was part of the law of England; and three years later, in the leading case of *Heathfield v. Chilton* (reported in 4 Burrow, p. 2015), Lord Chief Justice Mansfield reiterated his opinion, stating that,

> the privileges of public ministers and their retinue depend upon the law of nations; which is part of the common law of England. And the act of Parliament of 7 Ann. c. 12 did not intend to alter, nor can alter the law of nations.

The distinguished commentator, Sir William Blackstone, who had been counsel in both these cases tried before Lord Mansfield, wrote in the first edition of the fourth volume of his Commentaries upon the Laws of England, published in 1769, that:

> The law of nations (wherever any question arises which is properly the object of its jurisdiction) is here adopted in its full extent by the common law, and is held to be a

part of the law of the land. And those acts of Parliament, which have from time to time been made to enforce this universal law, or to facilitate the execution of its decisions, are not to be considered as introductive of any new rule, but merely as declaratory of the old fundamental constitutions of the Kingdom; without which it must cease to be a part of the civilized world.

In accordance with the views of English judges interpreting and applying the Common Law and in reliance upon the express language of the illustrious English commentator from whom they had learned their law, the Revolutionary statesmen of North America understood and stated that international law was a part of the law of the United States. Thus, Thomas Jefferson, Secretary of State under Washington's Administration, referred in the year 1793 to "the laws of the land, of which the law of nations makes an integral part." (American State Papers, Foreign Relations, Vol. 1, p. 150.) His great opponent, Alexander Hamilton, differing in most respects from Thomas Jefferson, nevertheless concurred in the view that international law was a part of the law of the land, and explained it more elaborately than Mr. Jefferson in the following passage quoted from the essays which Hamilton, under the pseudonym of Camillus, wrote for the Press in 1795 in defense of the Jay Treaty:

A question may be raised—Does this customary law of nations, as established in Europe, bind the United States? An affirmative answer to this is warranted by conclusive reasons.

1. The United States, when a member of the British Empire, were, in this capacity, a party to that law, and not having dissented from it, when they became independent, they are to be considered as having continued a party to it.

2. The common law of England, which was and is in force in each of these States, adopts the law of nations, the positive equally with the natural, as a part of itself.

3. Ever since we have been an independent nation, we have appealed to and acted upon the *modern* law of nations, as understood in Europe—various resolutions of Congress during our Revolution, the correspondence of executive officers, the decisions of our courts of admiralty, all recognize this standard.

4. Executive and legislative acts, and the proceedings of our courts, under the present government, speak a similar language. The President's proclamation of neutrality refers expressly to the *modern* law of nations, which must necessarily be understood as that prevailing in Europe, and acceded to by this country; and the general voice of our nation, together with the very arguments used against the treaty, accord in the same point. It is indubitable, that the customary law of European nations is as a part of the common law, and, by adoption, that of the United States. (Lodge's "Works of Alexander Hamilton," 1885, Vol. V, pp. 89-90.)

A recent decision of the Supreme Court of the United States defines the relation of international law to the law of the land as it was stated by Sir William Blackstone in his Commentaries published before the American Revolution. Thus, in the case of *The Paquete Habana* (reported in 175 United States Reports, pp. 677, 700), decided in 1899, Mr. Justice Gray, delivering the opinion of the Court, said:

> International law is part of our law, and must be ascertained and administered by the courts of justice of appropriate jurisdiction, as often as questions of right depending upon it are duly presented for their determination. For this purpose, where there is no treaty, and no controlling executive or legislative act or judicial decision, resort must be had to the customs and usages of civilized nations; and, as evidence of these, to the works of jurists and commentators, who, by years of labor, research, and experience, have made themselves peculiarly well acquainted with the subjects of which they treat. Such works are resorted to by judicial tribunals, not for the speculations of their authors concerning what the law ought to be but for trustworthy evidence of what the law really is.

It may be said in summing up the relation of international law to the common law of England and to the municipal law of the United States, that international law is part of the English common law; that as such it passed with the English colonies to America; that when, in consequence of successful rebellion, they were admitted to the society of nations, the new Republic recognized international law as completely as international law recognized the new Republic. Municipal law it was in England; municipal law it remained and is in the United States. Without expressing an opinion upon the vexed question whether it is law in the abstract, the courts, State and Federal, take judicial cognizance of its existence, and in appropriate cases enforce it, so that for the American student or practitioner international is domestic or municipal law.

The constitutions of certain Latin-American States expressly lay down the principle of Anglo-American law that international law is part of the law of the land. Thus, Article 106 of the constitution of the Dominican Republic and Article 125 of the constitution of Venezuela, which admits the principle with certain limitations. The constitution of Colombia of 1863 expressly declared that "The law of nations forms part of the national legislation," and an eminent American publicist specially versed in such matters states that "the authorities of the country are understood, in their treatment of neutrality and other questions, to have acknowledged the continuing force of the principle." In other constitutions of the American Republics the principle is not stated in express terms. It is, however, recognized implicitly or for specific cases; for example, Articles 31, 100, and 101 of the constitution of Argentina; Articles 59, 60, and 61 of the constitution of Brazil; Article 73 of the constitution of Chile; Article 107 of the constitution of Honduras; Article 96 of the constitution of Uruguay, etc., etc.

The laws of Latin-American countries—notably those relating to judicial procedure or to the organization of judicial authority—recognize, expressly or implicitly, the principle in question. In all the American countries the rules of international law have been treated as in force in their proclamations of neutrality in the great European war.

In future it must be expressly admitted as the basis of the public law of the New World that international law is part of the national legislation of every country. This is not only a principle of justice but one that is necessary to facilitate and to strengthen the friendly relations of all States.

The following impressive language of an eminent citizen of the American continent, Daniel Webster, to be found in an official instruction written when he was Secretary of State of the United States of America, may be quoted as a statement in summary form of the rights and duties of nations, especially of the American Republics:

> Every nation, on being received, at her own request, into the circle of civilized governments, must understand that she not only attains rights of sovereignty and the dignity of national character, but that she binds herself to the strict and faithful observance of all those principles, laws, and usages which have obtained currency among civilized states, and which have for their object the mitigation of the miseries of war.

REMARKS AT THE CLOSING SESSION OF THE AMERICAN INSTITUTE OF INTERNATIONAL LAW, JANUARY 8, 1916.

There must, gentlemen, be an end to all things, and the time has come for the Institute to adjourn, but not to close, its labors. Indeed, I might rather say that the time has come, or will come with the adjournment, to begin the serious work which has drawn us together and which we hope will justify our existence. A few days ago, when we met for the first time, we came together as publicists from the different countries of America deeply interested in international law and impressed with the belief that direction could be properly given to our efforts by a central organization, such as the American Institute of International Law. We close our session today as members of an organization embracing the publicists of the American continent. We have defined the objects, the aims and the purposes of the Institute, and the means whereby they may be realized. We have considered the relations that should exist between the Institute on the one hand and the twenty-one national societies of international law on the other and have found them to consist in coöperation under a central direction. We have completed the election of members of the Institute by selecting in each instance the five publicists recommended by the national societies for membership in the Institute. We have chosen the officers and we have agreed upon a method of procedure.

These facts would in themselves have justified the session, but we have done more than that. We have placed international law upon firm and larger foundations. We have adopted principles of justice which must and will regulate the relations of nations, if those relations are to be peaceful, as they will assuredly be if based upon principles of justice. We have adopted a declaration of the rights and duties of nations, to which we have prefixed a preamble stating the reasons for the declaration and a commentary justifying each one of the articles. In so doing, we have confessed our faith in justice as the one great concern of nations, as it is the one great concern of people within national lines, and we have expressed within the compass of half a dozen articles the fundamental principles upon which a stately and adequate structure of international law can be raised.

But we do not intend to content ourselves with the adoption of this declaration. We must strive by all the influence which we possess to make it a reality and to make it the measure of right and wrong in the relations of the American Republics one with another. The declaration of the rights and duties of nations is peculiarly an American document. It speaks not alone of rights, but it couples them with duties, because in any just conception right and duty are correlative, coexistent and coextensive, and, where peoples of the past have been prone to assert their rights, we are bold enough to proclaim our duties. We believe in the substitution of law for force, and that in this western continent law should control the conduct of states as well as the actions of men.

We have therefore stated the rights and duties of nations, not in terms of philosophy or of ethics, but in terms of law, and we have supported and justified each of the six articles forming the declaration by an adjudged case of the Supreme Court of the United States, thus asserting that these principles are law, that they have been and therefore can be administered in courts of justice; and we furthermore express the hope and confess our faith in the fact that they will be considered as law by the American Republics, that they will be applied in their mutual relations and that they will be interpreted, defined and developed in courts of justice, as, in the last resort, courts of justice must pass upon the actions of nations just as they pass upon the actions of men. We have shown by the adoption of the declaration that we believe in international law as a branch of jurisprudence, and the adoption of the declaration makes it possible to consider, to study, to expound and to develop it as such—a result which would indeed justify publicists in coming from all of the American Republics.

With the acceptance of the Declaration of the Rights and Duties of Nations the American Institute is in a position to take up and to consider in the light of fundamental principles of justice the various projects which have been submitted by its members during the session and especially the projects presented by the National Societies.

These will be referred to a commission in order that they may be examined as their importance deserves and, accompanied by a Report, they will be transmitted to the National Societies and laid before the next session of the Institute for such action as its members may, in their wisdom and in the fulness of knowledge, be minded to take.

In separating, we should have the consciousness that we have meant well and that we have done well. We have moreover the very great satisfaction of knowing that our acts have met with the approval not merely of the members who have taken part in the session but that they have excited the interest and expectation of the countries to which our members belong. For have we not been invited by the Government of Cuba during the course of this session to hold the next session of the Institute in the City of Havana as the guests of the nation? We have accepted this courteous invitation in the hope that we may prove to be not unworthy of the consideration shown us, and, in declaring the first session of the American Institute closed, I express the hope that we shall all meet in the City of Havana in the Republic of Cuba in the year 1917.

APPENDIX

Appendix

CONSTITUTION OF THE AMERICAN INSTITUTE OF INTERNATIONAL LAW

ARTICLE I. *Name*

An association is founded to be known as the *American Institute of International Law.*

ARTICLE II. *Object*

The American Institute of International Law is an unofficial scientific association.

It proposes:

1. To give precision to the general principles of international law as they now exist, or to formulate new ones, in conformity with the solidarity which unites the members of the society of civilized nations, in order to strengthen these bonds and, especially, the bonds between the American peoples;

2. To study questions of international law, particularly questions of an American character, and to endeavor to solve them, either in conformity with generally accepted principles, or by extending and developing them, or by creating new principles adapted to the special needs of the American Continent;

3. To discover a method of codifying the general or special principles of international law, and to elaborate projects of codification on matters which lend themselves thereto;

4. To aid in bringing about the triumph of the principles of justice and of humanity which should govern the relations between peoples, considered as nations, through more extensive instruction in international law, particularly in American universities, through lectures and addresses, as well as through publications and all other means;

5. To organize the study of international law along truly scientific and practical lines in a way that meets the needs of modern life, and taking into account the problems of our hemisphere and American doctrines;

6. To contribute, within the limits of its competence and the means at its disposal, toward the maintenance of peace, or toward the observance of the laws of war and the mitigation of the evils thereof;

. 7. To increase the sentiment of fraternity among the Republics of the American Continent, so as to strengthen friendship and mutual confidence among the citizens of the countries of the New World.

ARTICLE III.   *Membership*

The American Institute of International Law is composed of committees or delegates of the national societies of international law established in the different American Republics, which are affiliated therewith and of which it is the permanent representative.

It comprises:

1. Charter members;
2. Titular members;
3. Ex officio members;
4. Corresponding members.

The charter members are those who accepted this designation by signing, in 1912, the draft which has now become the present Constitution.

The titular members, chosen exclusively from among the publicists of the different Republics of the American Continent, are elected by the Institute, in conformity with the next article.   No Republic may have more than five such members at one and the same time.

If the secretary general of the national society of international law in any one of the American Republics is not personally a member of the Institute, he becomes of right a member ex officio, that is to say, by virtue of and for the term of his office.   Ex officio members have, as such, the same rights as titular members.

Jurists of non-American nationality, who, through their writings or their activity, shall have contributed to the progress of international law, may be elected corresponding members.

Corresponding members are invited to attend all the sessions of the Institute, with the same rights and privileges as American members. They have not, however, the right to vote either on administrative or scientific questions.

They are called upon to give their opinion on questions submitted to the consideration of the Institute, and they are active collaborators thereof.

They are exempt from the entrance fee and annual dues.

No one State can have more than three such members.

ARTICLE IV. *National Societies*

The national societies organized in each American Republic for the study and popularization of international law, whose members are jurists versed in international law, may affiliate with the American Institute. The members of these societies are entitled to attend the sessions of the Institute, but they may not take part in its deliberations nor may they vote.

The affiliated national societies propose duly qualified persons from among their nationals, for election as titular members by the Institute.

The members of the national societies, who are members of the Institute, constitute, in their country, a governing committee of the said society, which committee is the intellectual bond between the national society and the Institute.

The committee communicates, either directly, or through the secretary general of the national society, with the secretary general of the Institute, and sends him all the transactions and projects of the said society or informs him of the progress that has been made upon them.

The secretary general of the Institute transmits these transactions and projects in full, in part, or a synopsis thereof to the different national societies.

ARTICLE V. *Officers*

The officers of the Institute are an honorary president, a president, a secretary general, and a treasurer.

Before the close of each session there is an election of an honorary president and a president, who remain in office until the election of their successors at the following session.

The application of the foregoing second paragraph is provisionally suspended until the Institute shall have decided otherwise.

In the elections individual ballots are cast, and only the members present are permitted to vote. Nevertheless, absent members are allowed to send their votes in writing, in sealed envelopes. Candidates must receive a majority of the votes of the members present, as well as a majority of all the votes validly cast, in order to be elected.

ARTICLE VI. *Executive Council*

An *Executive Council* is the governing body of the Institute.

It meets at Washington, the seat of the Institute.

It is composed of the president, the secretary general, and the treasurer, who are members ex officio, and of two other members elected at the beginning of each session. They are eligible for re-election.

It has the right to increase its membership and itself elects additional members, if it deems it necessary.

ARTICLE VII. *Secretary General*

The secretary general is elected by the Institute for three sessions. He is eligible for re-election.

He has in his charge the drafting of the minutes of each meeting, all the publications of the Institute, its routine work, its correspondence, and the execution of its decisions, unless the Institute provides otherwise. He is keeper of its seal and of its archives. At the beginning of each session he presents a summary of the work of the preceding session.

ARTICLE VIII. *Assistant Secretaries*

On the proposal of the secretary general, the Institute may appoint one or more assistant secretaries, to aid him in the performance of his duties or to represent him in his absence.

ARTICLE IX. *Treasurer*

The treasurer is elected for three sessions. He is eligible for re-election.

He has in his charge the financial affairs of the Institute, under the control of the Executive Council. He presents a detailed report at each session.

Two members are designated at the first meeting as auditors, and present, during the session, a report on the result of their examination of the treasurer's accounts.

ARTICLE X. *Reporters*

The Executive Council submits questions for examination and study to the affiliated national societies, or appoints reporters from among its members, or organizes committees for the preparatory study of questions that are to be submitted to the deliberations of the Institute.

In urgent cases, the secretary general himself prepares the reports.

ARTICLE XI. *Sessions*

There shall be at least one session of the Institute every two years; but the Executive Council may, during this interval, call an extra session of the Institute.

At each session the Institute designates the place and the time of the following session. It may leave this designation to the Executive Council.

ARTICLE XII.　*Languages*

French, the language of the *Institut de droit international* and of the Peace Conferences, is likewise the language of the Institute.

Nevertheless the use of Spanish, Portuguese, and English, as national languages, is permitted as of right.

Every official document that is to be published is translated into the language or languages selected by the officers.

ARTICLE XIII.　*Publication of Proceedings*

After each session, the Institute publishes an account of its proceedings.

ARTICLE XIV.　*Dues and Funds*

The expenses of the Institute are covered:

1. By the dues of its members, as well as by an entrance fee.

The dues are, unless the by-laws provide to the contrary, an entrance fee of ten dollars and annual dues of five dollars. The dues are payable from and including the year of election. They entitle the member to all the publications of the Institute. An unjustifiable delay of more than three years in the payment of dues may be considered as equivalent to a resignation.

2. By foundations and other gifts.

It is proposed that a fund be gradually formed, the income from which shall be devoted to the expenses of the sessions, of the publications, of the secretariat, and of other routine matters.

ARTICLE XV.　*Amendments.*

The present constitution may be revised or amended, in whole or in part, at a regular session, on the request of a majority of the members present and voting.

BY-LAWS OF THE AMERICAN INSTITUTE OF INTERNATIONAL LAW

PART I

Members

ARTICLE I

The titular members of the Institute are elected by it from the list of names presented by the affiliated national society.

ARTICLE II

Where no affiliated national society exists or where the existing society neglects to present candidates, the Institute provides for nominations or vacancies as it sees fit.

ARTICLE III

Corresponding members are elected by the Institute on the proposal of the Executive Council, at the meeting devoted to the election of titular members.

PART II

Preliminary Work between Sessions

ARTICLE IV

By article X of the Constitution the Executive Council presents the questions for study, either by laying them before the national societies, or by designating two reporters, or one reporter and a committee of study for each question.

In the former case, the subject, with or without a questionnaire, is submitted to each national society.

If two reporters are appointed, each of them prepares a memorandum, after which one of them or a third reporter designated by the Executive Council prepares a report on the basis of and with the assistance of the memoranda presented.

If a reporter and a committee of study are designated, the reporter must get into communication with the members of the committee before the 31st of December of the year of his appointment, and submit his ideas to them and learn their views.

Every member, who signifies his desire to that effect, has the right to be a member of such of the committees of study as he shall indicate to the secretary general.

ARTICLE V

The national societies and the reporters must transmit their studies or reports to the secretary general in ample time for their publication and distribution before the session at which they are to be discussed.

The secretary general does not provide for the printing or distribution of other reports or documents prepared by the reporters or by members of committees or of the Institute. Such works are published only in exceptional cases and by virtue of an express decision on the part of the Institute or the Executive Council.

PART III
Sessions
ARTICLE VI

There may be no more than one session each year. The interval between two sessions must not exceed two years.

At each session the Institute designates the place and time of the next session. This designation may be left to the Executive Council (Constitution, Article XI). In this case, the secretary general informs the national societies affiliated with the Institute, at least four months in advance, of the place and date determined upon.

ARTICLE VII

The program of the session is drawn up by the Executive Council, and the secretary general brings it to the attention of the national societies as soon as possible.

The program must be accompanied by the summary of the progress made on the preparatory work, as well as by all other information that may facilitate the labors of the members taking part in the session.

ARTICLE VIII

Members who desire to propose new questions for study are invited to lay them before the Executive Council at the beginning of the session. This invitation must be extended by the president at the opening of the sessions.

ARTICLE IX

The president, after consultation with the Executive Council and the reporters, determines the order in which the subjects should be treated; but the program is in all cases under the control of the Assembly itself.

PART IV

Meetings

ARTICLE X

The meetings are devoted to scientific work.

The titular members and the corresponding members take part in them. The former have the right to vote; the latter have the right merely to take part in the discussions.

The meetings are not public. The Executive Council may, however, permit the attendance of the local authorities and press, as well as of persons who request to be admitted.

ARTICLE XI

Unless otherwise resolved by a special decision of the Executive Council, the president delivers an address immediately after the opening of the first meeting.

The secretary general presents a summary of the work of the last session and makes known the names of the assistant secretaries or editors whom he has appointed to aid him in drawing up the minutes of the session.

The assistant secretaries or editors hold office only during the session.

ARTICLE XII

The treasurer is then requested to present his accounts to the Institute, and two auditors are thereupon elected to examine the accounts of the treasurer. The auditors present their report in the course of the session (Constitution, Art. IX).

ARTICLE XIII

Each meeting is opened by the reading of the minutes of the preceding meeting.

Separate minutes are drawn up for each meeting, even when there are more than one on the same day; but the minutes of the morning meeting are read only at the opening of the next day's meeting.

The members present approve or revise the minutes. Revision can be requested only in the matter of wording, of errors, or of omissions. A decision cannot be changed in the minutes.

The minutes of the last meeting of a session are approved by the president.

ARTICLE XIV

If the Executive Council deems it advisable to consider a matter as urgent, it may propose the immediate discussion thereof, and, if the majority of the members present agree, the matter may be put to vote in the course of this session; otherwise the proposition is of right postponed until the following session.

ARTICLE XV

Committees may be appointed during a meeting for the examination of certain questions. These committees may, in turn, appoint sub-committees.

ARTICLE XVI

The propositions of the reporters and of the committees form the basis of the deliberations in the meetings.

The members of committees have the right to complete and develop their individual opinions.

ARTICLE XVII

The discussion is then opened. It takes place in the languages indicated in Article XII of the constitution.

At the request of the members, the discussion may be summed up in French.

ARTICLE XVIII

No one may speak without having been previously recognized by the president.

The latter notes the names of the members who request the floor and recognizes them in the order of their requests.

The reporters, however, when the question on which they have made a report is under discussion, are not subject to the rule of speaking in turn. The same is true of the president of the committee.

ARTICLE XIX

The reading of an address is forbidden, unless specially authorized by the president.

ARTICLE XX

If a speaker digresses too far from the subject under consideration, the president calls his attention to the fact and requests him to speak to the question.

ARTICLE XXI

All propositions and all amendments are submitted, in writing, to the president.

ARTICLE XXII

If a point of order is raised during a deliberation, the discussion of the main question is suspended until the assembly passes upon the point of order.

ARTICLE XXIII

The closing of the discussion may be proposed. The discussion may not, however, be declared closed, unless a two-thirds majority of the assembly so votes.

If no one demands the floor or if it has been resolved to close the discussion, the president declares the discussion closed. Thereafter no one may be given the floor, except, in special cases, the reporter or the president of the committee.

ARTICLE XXIV

Before proceeding to a vote, the president submits to the assembly the order in which the questions will be voted upon.

If there are objections to the order, the assembly passes upon them at once.

ARTICLE XXV

Amendments to amendments are put to vote before amendments, and the latter before the main question. Proposals purely and simply to reject the question are not considered amendments.

Where there are more than two alternate main propositions, they are all put to vote, one after the other, and every member may vote for one of them. When a vote has thus been taken on all the propositions, if none of them has obtained a majority, the members decide, by another ballot, which of the two propositions receiving the least number of votes must be eliminated. The remaining propositions are then voted upon in the same manner until only one is left, upon which a definitive vote may be taken.

ARTICLE XXVI

The adoption of an amendment to an amendment does not bind a member to vote for the amendment itself; neither does the adoption of an amendment obligate a member to vote in favor of the main proposition.

ARTICLE XXVII

When a proposition is capable of being divided, any member may request a vote by division.

ARTICLE XXVIII

When the proposition under consideration is drawn up in several articles, the proposition as a whole is first subjected to general discussion.

After such discussion and the vote on its articles, the proposition as a whole is put to vote. Such vote may be postponed until a subsequent meeting.

ARTICLE XXIX

The voting is done by raising the hand.

No one is bound to take part in a vote. If some of the members present abstain, the question is decided by the majority of those voting.

In case of a tie, the proposition is considered defeated.

ARTICLE XXX

The vote may be taken by roll-call, if five members so request. There is always occasion for a roll-call on a scientific proposition as a whole.

The minutes mention the names of the members voting for or against and the names of those who abstain.

Article XXXI

The Institute may decide that a second deliberation should take place, either in the course of the session, or during the following session, or that its decisions be referred to a drafting committee to be designated by itself or by the Executive Council.

OFFICERS AND MEMBERS OF THE AMERICAN INSTITUTE OF INTERNATIONAL LAW

OFFICERS

ELIHU ROOT, *Honorary President*
JAMES BROWN SCOTT, *President*
ALEJANDRO ALVAREZ, *Secretary General*
LUIS ANDERSON, *Treasurer*

EXECUTIVE COUNCIL

ELIHU ROOT
JAMES BROWN SCOTT
ALEJANDRO ALVAREZ
LUIS ANDERSON
ANTONIO SANCHEZ DE BUSTAMANTE
JOAQUIN D. CASASUS[1]

PERMANENT COMMITTEE FOR THE STUDY OF QUESTIONS RELATING TO NEUTRALITY

The Executive Council

CHARTER MEMBERS

Argentine Republic: LUIS M. DRAGO
Bolivia: ALBERTO GUTIERREZ
Brazil: RUY BARBOSA
Chile: ALEJANDRO ALVAREZ
Colombia: ANTONIO JOSÉ URIBE
Costa Rica: LUIS ANDERSON
Cuba: ANTONIO SANCHEZ DE BUSTAMANTE
Dominican Republic: ANDRÉS J. MONTOLIO
Ecuador: RAFAEL ARIZAGA
Guatemala: ANTONIO BATRES JAUREGUI
Haiti: J. N. LÉGER
Honduras: ALBERTO MEMBREÑO
Mexico: JOAQUIN D. CASASUS (Deceased)

---

[1]Died February 25, 1916.

Nicaragua: SALVADOR CASTRILLO
Panama: FEDERICO BOYD
Paraguay: MANUEL GONDRA
Peru: RAMON RIBEYRO
Salvador: RAFAEL S. LOPEZ (deceased)
United States of America: JAMES BROWN SCOTT
Uruguay: CARLOS M. DE PENA
Venezuela: JOSÉ GIL FORTOUL

TITULAR MEMBERS

Argentine Republic

EDUARDO BIDAU
CARLOS OCTAVIO BUNGE
LUIS M. DRAGO
JOAQUIN V. GONZALEZ
EDUARDO SARMIENTO LASPIUR

Bolivia

DANIEL SANCHEZ BUSTAMANTE
ALBERTO GUTIERREZ
ALBERTO DIEZ DE MEDINA
CLAUDIO PINILLA
VICTOR E. SANJÍNES

Brazil

CLOVIS BEVILAQUA
LAURO MÜLLER
RODRIGO OCTAVIO
MANOEL CICERO PERERGINO DA SILVA
EPITACIO PESSOA

Chile

ALEJANDRO ALVAREZ
LUIS BARROS BORGOÑO
ANTONIO HUNEEUS
EDUARDO SUAREZ MUJICA
ELIODORO YAÑES

Colombia

NICOLAS ESGUERRA
ANTONIO JOSÉ URIBE
FRANCISCO JOSÉ URRUTIA
ADOLFO URUETA
JOSÉ MARIA GONZALEZ VALENCIA

Costa Rica

LUIS ANDERSON
RICARDO GIMENES
LEONIDAS PACHECO
MANUEL CASTRO QUESADA
C. GONZALEZ VIQUES

Cuba

ANTONIO SANCHEZ DE BUSTAMANTE
PABLO DESVERNINE
OCTAVIO GIBERGA
FERNANDO SANCHEZ DE FUENTES
RAFAEL MONTORO

Dominican Republic

FEDERICO HENRIQUES CARVAJAL
MANUEL J. TRONCOSO DE LA CONCHA
MANUEL ARTURO MACHADO
ANDRES J. MONTOLIO
ADOLFO ALEJANDRO NOUEL

Ecuador

RAFAEL MARÍA ARIZAGA
ALEJANDRO CARDENAS
GONZALO S. CÓRDOVA
VICTOR MANUEL PEÑAHERRERA
JOSÉ LUIS TAMAYO

Guatemala

MARIANO CRUZ
ANTONIO BATRES JÁUREGUI
JOSÉ MATOS
ALBERTO MENCOS
CARLOS SALAZAR

Haiti

Louis Borno
Edmond Héraux
Pierre Hudicourt
Jacques N. Léger
Solon Ménos

Honduras

Fausto Davila
Alberto Membreño
Alberto Uclés
Ricardo de J. Urrutia
Mariano Vásquez

Mexico

Francisco L. de la Barra
Manuel Calero
Joaquin D. Casasus[1]
Victor Manuel Castillo
Pedro Lascurain

Nicaragua

Modesto Barrios
Alejandro Cesar
Pedro Gonzalez
Carlos Cuadra Pasos
Maximo H. Zepeda

Panama

Ricardo J. Alfaro
Harmodio Arias
Eusebio A. Morales
Belisario Porras
Ramon M. Valdes

Paraguay

Eusebio Ayala
Cecilio Baez
Manuel Gondra
Antolin Irala
Fulgencio R. Moreno

---

[1]Died February 25, 1916.

Peru

ISAAC ALZAMORA
VICTOR M. MAURTUA
SOLON POLO
RAMON RIBEYRO
MANUEL V. VILLARÁN

Salvador

SALVADOR GALLEGOS
ALONSO REYES GUERRA
VICTOR JEREZ
MANUEL I. MORALES
FRANCISCO MARTINEZ SUAREZ

United States of America

ROBERT BACON
ROBERT LANSING
ELIHU ROOT
LEO S. ROWE
JAMES BROWN SCOTT

Uruguay

DANIEL GARCIA ACEVEDO
MANUEL ARBELAIZ
JUAN ANTONIO BUERO
ADOLFO BERRO GARCIA
JUAN ZORILLA DE SAN MARTIN

Venezuela

SIMON BARCELÓ
ARMINIO BORJAS
JESUS ROJAS FERNANDEZ
JOSÉ GIL FORTOUL
F. ARROYO PAREJO

Other Books by James Brown Scott Published by The Lawbook Exchange, Ltd.

The Catholic Conception of International Law. Francisco de Vitoria, Founder of the Modern Law of Nations. Francisco Suarez, Founder of the Modern Philosophy of Law in General and in Particular of the Laws of Nations. A Critical Examination and a Justified Appreciation. Washington, D.C.: Georgetown University Press, 1934. [xviii], 494 pp. **With a new introduction by William E. Butler, John Edward Fowler Distinguished Professor of Law, Pennsylvania State University; Academician, National Academy of Sciences of Ukraine and Russian Academy of Natural Sciences.** ISBN-13: 9781584778219. Hardcover, 2008. Book # 48728.

Reprint of the sole edition. This important study of international law theory before Grotius discusses the work of Victoria and Suarez, together with the writings of later Catholic jurists of the period, such as Mariana, Buchanan and Bellarmine. Contemporary Protestant jurists are discussed as well. "The outstanding merit of the book for which Dr. Scott has placed scholars and lawyers in his debt is that it is a needed reminder that the ideas and conceptions on which the internal order of states, no less than the good order of the international community, depend, are not of today nor of yesterday, but that they have a long history, and that their deepest roots are in the great tradition of Christian thought, which, through the centuries, was elaborated by schoolmen and canonists and jurists with a power of analysis and insight which puts to shame the contributions of much of what passes for contemporary jurisprudence.": John Dickinson, *Georgetown Law Journal* 24 (1935-36) 218.

James Madison's Notes of Debates in the Federal Convention of 1787 and their Relation to a More Perfect Society of Nations. New York: Oxford University Press, 1918. xviii, 149pp. ISBN-13: 9781584771647. Hardcover, 2001. Book # 30768.

Scott examines Madison's notes on the Federal Convention of 1787 from the perspective that the Federal Convention of 1787 "was in fact as well as in form an international conference" (from the Preface) and therefore views the Constitution as an international document. Henry Wolf Bikle called the work "an excellent resume of the history of the Federal Convention of 1787, primarily in the light of Madison's *Notes of the Debates*.": *Harvard Law Review* 33:744.

Judicial Settlement of Controversies between States of the American Union: An Analysis of Cases Decided in the Supreme Court of the United States. Oxford: Clarendon Press, 1919. xiii, 548 pp. ISBN-13: 9781584771722. Hardcover, 2002. Book # 33607.

This volume offers the texts of eighty Supreme Court decisions written between 1799 and 1918 concerning controversies between states, along with extensive analyses and commentaries. These are preceded by three general chapters that examine the rise of judicial procedure between the states, the ability of states to be sued by citizens of other states, and attempts by citizens of states to bring action against other states by methods of indirection. As indicated by the final chapter, "A Lesson For the World at Large," the author has a larger goal in mind. Deeply influenced by the devastation of the First World War, Scott [1866-1943], a participant in the Versailles Conference, aimed to demonstrate that the American legal system that maintains peace between the individual states could serve as a model for the rest of the world.

Law, The State, and the International Community. New York: Columbia University Press, 1939-1940. 2 Vols. ISBN-13: 9781584771784. Hardcover, 2002. Book # 55780.

Volume One: A Commentary on the Development of Legal, Political and International Ideals. Volume Two: Extracts Illustrating the Growth of Theories, and Principles of Jurisprudence, Government, and The Law of Nations. "This is a work of ambitious scope and conspicuous industry. It attempts a survey of the chief currents of political and juridical speculation from classical times to the end of the 16th century. The author divides his subject into six main periods: The Greek Background, The Roman Heritage, The Christian Heritage (Ancient and Medieval), The Transition from Medieval to Modern Thought, The Era of Reform, The Beginning of the Modern Age. The terminus is Richard Hooker on the brink of the 17th century. From the Dark Ages onwards, the teachings of twenty celebrated theological, political, and international savants are analyzed and presented in concentrated form. (...) One of Professor Scott's best chapters is on Francisco de Vittoria (c. 1483-1546), who is of particular interest for his influence on Grotius, and to whose remarkable Relectio de Indis Professor Scott has devoted special research."

Sovereign States and Suits Before Arbitral Tribunals and Courts of Justice. New York: New York University Press, 1925. x, 360 pp. ISBN-13: 9781584774594. Hardcover, 2004. Book # 40000.

This book grew out of a series of lectures delivered at New York University in 1924. Scott outlines a history of states gradually renouncing warfare in favor of international mediating agencies. His conclusions were overly optimistic, but his book remains valuable for its intellectual history of inter-state mediation and its insights into the relationship between sovereign states and the Hague Tribunal of Arbitration and the Permanent Court of International Justice.

The Spanish Origin of International Law. Francisco De Vitoria and His Law of Nations. London: Humphrey Milford, 1934. 19a, 288, clviii pp. Frontispiece and portrait. ISBN-13: 9781-584771104. Hardcover, 2000. Book # 28762.
Francisco de Vitoria [c. 1483-1546] is widely considered to be a founder of international law. Scott holds that Vitoria's 16th century school of international law and his important *Reflectiones, De Indis Noviter Inventis* and *De Jure Belli* (the text of these are included in the appendix) are in fact the origin of the law of nations, which was to become the international law of Christendom and the world at large. In Vitoria's writings described herein he held that pagans had the right to freedom and property, declared slavery to be unsound, upheld the rights of Indians, questioned the Spanish conquest of the New World, which gave rise to his thesis that the community of nations transcends Christendom.

The United States of America: A Study in International Organization. New York: Oxford University Press, 1920. xix, 605 pp. ISBN-13: 9781584771715. Hardcover, 2003. Book # 33674.
With an extensive appendix of source readings. Scott presents a detailed and comprehensively documented history of the American Constitution from its roots in the Mayflower Compact and other colonial associations through the Eighteenth Amendment. A survey history, his study is especially interesting as a political document written to address the effects of the First World War. Scott wrote this book for a European audience, hoping that his analysis of the Constitution would influence the creation of an international organization of states governed by a "Court of Nations" modeled on the American Supreme Court. He emphasizes the Constitution's role as an agent of peace and cooperation among different political units. His ideas were later reflected in the establishment of the International Court of Justice, the League of Nations and the United Nations.

The Lawbook Exchange, Ltd. 33 Terminal Avenue, Clark, NJ 07066
732-382-1800   1-800-422-6686   www.lawbookexchange.com

www.ingramcontent.com/pod-product-compliance
Lightning Source LLC
Chambersburg PA
CBHW031936190326
41519CB00007B/556